Emmalea

TWICE LOVED

ROSALYN ROGERS-HAMRICK

ISBN 978-1-64258-113-3 (paperback)
ISBN 978-1-64258-114-0 (digital)

Copyright © 2018 by Rosalyn Rogers-Hamrick

All rights reserved. No part of this publication may be reproduced, distributed, or transmitted in any form or by any means, including photocopying, recording, or other electronic or mechanical methods without the prior written permission of the publisher. For permission requests, solicit the publisher via the address below.

Christian Faith Publishing, Inc.
832 Park Avenue
Meadville, PA 16335
www.christianfaithpublishing.com

The story, all names, characters, and incidents portrayed in this book are fictitious. No identification with actual persons, places, buildings, and products, is intended or should be inferred.

Printed in the United States of America

Dedication

ENCOURAGEMENT IS DEFINED BY WEBSTER'S as "the action of giving someone support, confidence, or hope." With a grateful heart, I thank my loving husband, James, of forty-six years, for his *encouragement* regarding my writing *Emmalea*. His example as a godly man is outstanding. His example as a published author himself made my writing a breeze!

Direction is defined by *Webster's* as "a guiding, governing, or motivating purpose." With all that I am, I thank my Heavenly Father for his direction and for him trusting me with his *Emmalea* project.

There are four others I must mention—the *first* being the late Charlie Smith. Many years ago, he was my boss when I worked at Equifax-PMI in Charleston, West Virginia. He once told me that whatever I would choose to do in life, he just knew that I would be good at it. His vote of confidence, I have never forgotten.

Also Bob and the two sisters-in-law at Gulf Shores, Alabama. You know who you are! Hey…I did it, thanks!

Acknowledgments

James J. Hamrick   *Inside Illustrator*

Cimperman & Co. Photography
33 Vine Avenue Sharon PA 16146   *Author's Portrait*
724-342-6131

Preface   *By Author*

Daniel Webster's Dictionary   *Definitions*

Bible Quotes   *New King James Bible*

Contents

Preface 9

Introduction 11

One   Location, Location, Location! 13

Two   Twenty-Five Years Earlier (It Was the '90s!) 34

Three   Young, Having Fun, Growing Up along the Way! 44

Four   Graduation! 62

Five   Leaving, aka Got to Go Now! 71

Six   Y2K…and Beyond! 75

Seven   Now What? 129

Eight   Meanwhile, Back in Madison! 169

Promised Recipes 195

Preface

I FIND IT FASCINATING THAT when a Christian gives God the *okay* to do something new in their lives, *he does just that!* That's the good news. The challenge is that his timing often comes *not* when you think you're ready but rather when he says you are.

With his two words "It's time!" came my retirement from a life of nursing and administration. To say the least, I had to make a few difficult decisions. One would require my husband and me to put our lives in storage and then set out on an American adventure—with our first stop being in Kansas City, Kansas. We spent a lovely Thanksgiving with our youngest son and his family.

It was during a routine gas stop that I saw a field of white crosses. That image overwhelmed me, so much, that I became choked up and speechless. From that one moment in time, the inspiration for *Emmalea* was birthed. I wept as I began telling my husband a brief overview of what you're about to read in the following eight chapters.

Who am I? Well, you know, I'm not a well-known writer, but now I write. I'm not a well-known anything. I'm just an average lady with an above-average capacity in finding enjoyment in hearing the life stories of others. Some has been full of lightheartedness, some are fun-loving, while others are too humorous for words. Most are full of honesty, and all have been full of both successes and failures.

What's your story? If we meet, I'd love to hear about it. Perhaps, just maybe, it will be the inspiration for my next book! In the meantime, enjoy *Emmalea*.

Introduction

LET ME BEGIN BY SAYING what *Emmalea* is not. It is not the obvious or the predictable. Some may even say it's somewhat controversial. *Emmalea* will challenge you to keep an open heart and an open mind throughout. *Emmalea* covers three generations of average Americans living with the day-to-day choices they have made.

As you are well aware, choices are categorized as either being good ones or poor ones. Most of our lives are made up of a good mix of both, and the lives of the characters in *Emmalea* are no different. When an unbalance occurs—oftentimes because a poor choice was made, whether made by a person or by someone else affecting that person—God has his way of restoring balance … through hope, love, and always through a pathway of forgiveness.

Statements like…"It's OK!" "Surprise!" "3,562" "Blue streaks!" "Y2K" "You're not the worst thing you've ever done!" "Rubik's Cube," "Love baked in a 325-degree oven," "Forgive," and "Denver sunsets" will all make sense to you as you read *Emmalea: TWICE LOVED*.

Chapter One

Location, Location, Location!

IF YOU SHOULD EVER FIND yourself traveling down Old Country Road 707 in Madison, Arkansas, you'd pass by Carol's Place. It's the only mom-and-pop diner–gas station combo in Harrison County. Directly across this local landmark, live Ben and Sally Rogers.

The Rogers are as unique as their rural mailbox. It was in the shape of a yellow birdhouse with a bright-green roof. Their mail carrier, Alvin Kane, only must lift its rooftop to deposit their mail. Ben and Sally's home was a modest two-story house with white wooden siding and a forest-green tin roof. The home's large front porch was so inviting, that visitors find it hard to resist. They either swing or rock their time and cares away while sipping on a glass of Sally's chilled apple cider when they stopped by.

Ben and Sally inherited this 142-acre farm from Sally's parents, Mr. and Mrs. Homer Glick, when they were a very young couple. It was Homer and Mary Anne that named this little piece of heaven Bethesda Acres Farm. Passersby knew this by reading the faded sign posted at the entrance to the Rogers' gravel drive.

Today Ben was busy spending his Saturday morning replacing several shingles that had blown off their old red barn roof during Thursday's powerful thunderstorm. WPQJ, local channel 13, reported that the wind was due to the El Niño weather pattern. Regardless of the cause, all Ben Rogers knew was that his barn needs fixin'.

Sally strongly suggested that he should hire it done. However, today Ben was thinking he was forty years old and would get the job done. Tomorrow, Sally knew, her husband's body would be reminding him that he was, in fact, fifty-five!

Ben said, "To a farmer, they're only numbers, and my obligations mean more than they do!"

So being the helpmate she is, Sally would place two ibuprofen capsules next to his glass of orange juice at the breakfast table, and their day would go on—a day full of details and deadlines. Modern-day farm life was the same now as it has always been, a good mix of whimsy and demands. Sally too, finds herself outdoors the larger part of her afternoons. She especially enjoyed the autumn season because it was her favorite time of the year. The planting and the harvesting were over, and both Ben and Sally were looking forward to some much-needed rest and time to plan for the next.

This year made thirty-one years that they had labored through planting and harvesting on Bethesda Acres. This had been successfully done only by embracing the farm's familiar cycles of dependability with a few uncertainties that might pop up along the way.

Speaking of familiarities, today being Saturday, Sally would start early in the morning baking four southern pecan pound cakes. She did this for her childhood friend, Carol West—the one and only Carol of Carol's Place. Carol sold them at her diner for $3 per slice, as she had done for nearly six years now! Sally's cakes were such a local favorite that they had become a staple in Madison's weekend dining experience.

I dare not forget to mention that they, too, were a sweet treat for those weary travelers that made their way to Carol's by taking Exit 4B off of the I-74 ramp then turning right toward the tiny town of Madison. A tank full of gas and their stomachs satisfied with Carol's daily specials—a fresh cup of high-test coffee along with a slice of Sally's down-on-the-farm goodness—I ask you, what more could a motorist ask for?

Three cakes were made to fulfill Carol's order, but as mentioned, Sally always made four. Why? Because she kept one for her Ben. Ben had had a long-standing joke with Carol—being he was relieved that he didn't have to pay her asking price of $3 per slice! This ongoing joke had kept their friendship lighthearted and Ben's wallet a little thicker too!

A cake all to himself! Well, rightfully so, because Ben harvested the nuts from their farm's pecan grove. Bethesda Acres grove was made up of twelve mature pecan trees. Sally enjoyed watching close by as Ben shook their tree limbs, causing the ripened nuts to fall to the ground. To her they looked like heavy brown snowflakes that made a funny thumping sound when they hit the ground instead of the usual snowflakes' silent fall.

Sally reminisced, thinking that their sound reminded her of Thumper—you know, the rabbit Thumper, thumping his foot in the movie *Bambi*. *Bambi* was the only movie her parents ever took her to see. They watched it at the Robinson Grand Theater when they traveled to Indianapolis to buy a combine from the John Deere dealership there. That fond childhood memory was one that she brought back to life every year at nut harvesttime—a tiny part of her history that brought her huge emotional benefits!

Sally lent Ben a helping hand in gathering the nuts for storing. Later, he'd crack as many as she would be needing. So every Friday evening, Ben could be found in one of two places. He'd be in front of the TV, watching a Western on cable while cracking pecans, or in his workshop located next to the barn, cracking them on his workbench.

By the way, if you've ever wondered what "home sweet home" smells like, all you have to do is drop in on Sally any given Saturday morning, and your question will be answered! And if you've ever wondered what it tastes like, stop in at Carol's, and for $3, your question will be answered too!

Ben just finished fixin' the barn roof. He put away his tools and ladder. Thirsty, he was going to the house for a cool glass of lemonade—not entering through Sally's kitchen door before thoroughly wiping off his boots on the rag rug that she had placed on the stoop (*just for him!*).

As Ben followed his nose inside, there stood his Sally. She was finishing off her pecan creations with a dusting of confectionary sugar. Her salt-and-pepper hair was just long enough to pull back into a ponytail. Today she tied it back with a purple ribbon. Her skin had the appearance of being kissed by Arkansas's Indian summer sun. And those brown eyes, along with her facial expressions, communicated with Ben without her lips having to utter a single word.

Ben became so overwhelmed with what he saw that he just had to say it;

"Sally, you are such a *good* woman to come home to!"

Well, that did it! Sally did a 360, turning her focus from her pound cakes onto her Ben. His endearing proclamation caused her heart to skip a beat so that she had to put her Bundt cake pan down and run over to give him one of the biggest hugs that he'd ever been given!

You see, there are times in a relationship that couples need to take extra-special pleasures in one another. These much-desired times don't have to cease to exist just because a couple is fifty-five-plus and now qualifies for senior discounts around town!

As their love flames were turned up, Ben and Sally's love story would continue. They both took the time to recognize and seize such moments of compassion that only the two of them had the right to share—not that others had never tried to overstep that boundary into their inner circle of love. Both Sally and Ben has had to put "those trespassers" in their rightful place—*outside*, where they belonged!

Sunday morning came quickly. Both their rooster and their alarm clock were competing for Ben and Sally's attention!

"Good morning, Ben!" "Good morning, Sally!" "Wake up, you two, wake up!" "Ben, who's going to greet the newcomers at church if you sleep in?" and "Sally, who's going to teach your Sunday school class if you sleep in?"

Ms. Sally, as she was known at church, enjoyed teaching, rocking, and cuddling her young students. Her floral tote was loaded down with age-appropriate toys and snacks. She also remembered to pack plenty of disinfectant wipes, because she'd surely be needing them! Sally had been assisting the parents of one of her students, two-year-old Wes Roberts, with potty training, and he was making excellent progress from week to week. Her only little girl student, three-and-a-half-year-old Melissa Gray, was so smart. Why, she could hardly sit still as she anxiously waited for story time to begin! Sally was certain that Melissa would become a well-known scholar when she grew up. And to think, it all began in her *class of four!*

Sally arranged her tiny students around the pine kiddie table. Wes was in the blue chair. Melissa was in the pink chair. Nathan was in the green chair, and Josiah sat down on the red one. Opening her Bible storybook, Sally turned to today's lesson located on page 14. She then placed a ziplock baggie full of animal crackers and animal cookies in the center of the table.

Now having her students' full attention, she instructed them, saying, "Class, today we'll be learning about Noah, his ark, and some of the animals in the ark."

"The ark is a very big boat" was the answer she gave to Melissa's first question of the day.

Ms. Sally continued by instructing her class that every time an animal was mentioned, they could reach in the baggie and pull out that animal to have as their snack.

Today her class particularly enjoyed learning about Noah and the animals, especially little Josiah Oliver. He was a cutie and full of mischief too!

As Ms. Sally read, "Two by two, the lions boarded the ark," he reached in, pulling out two lion crackers, biting off their tails.

Then he began to roar like lions do. The other students followed, roaring so loudly that her class became a lion's den! The classroom burst out into so much laughter that they could be heard by the passersby in the hallway. They began peeping their heads inside her door, wanting to join in on all the fun!

Sally planned on keeping her eyes on little Josiah. She was sure that once age bridled his mischievousness, he was destined to become a strong leader (perhaps even in the military). For now she'd just have to wait and see, as she prayed for him and his gift.

Fun and safe was what Ms. Sally's Sunday school class was known for. This welcomed fact gave the parents and loved ones of her students the freedom to learn by listening to the biblical teachings of Reverend Joseph Palmer. His preaching was biblically sound, as they pertained to the many ways the Lord cares for his people in their day-to-day lives, as well as for all eternity!

After today's closing prayer, and the last toddler had been handed over to their family member, Sally restored order to her classroom. She cleaned and disinfected the table, chairs, and toys. She emptied the trash and placed each book in their assigned place. With all chairs neatly placed under the kiddie table, it was lights out!

Sally met Ben in the church's upstairs foyer. He was talking with a new visiting couple. He turned and proudly introduced his wife to Jim and Marcy Jones. They both appeared to be in their late thirties to early forties. Their family recently moved to Madison from northern West Virginia, where they both graduated from West Virginia University. This week Jim took the new position as pharmacist at Mercer's Pharmacy on Main Street. Marcy said that she planned on doing some volunteer work at the new public library in nearby Verona.

Standing there watching Sally interact with the Jones reminded Ben how proud he was to call her his wife! Ben's pride in Sally Glick started as far back as he could remember. She'd just been awarded two blue ribbons at the Arkansas State Fair.

One was for her delicious canned sweet pickles and the other for a sunflower arrangement she had made from the sunflowers she had grown. Ben saved Sally a seat on the school bus, insisting that she showed everyone her first-place ribbons! All that fuss, even before the bus driver had a chance to take his foot off the brake and place it onto the gas pedal.

Tall, rough hands, John Deere cap, blue jeans, and wearing a brown plaid shirt, Ben was so country cool. Cool and thoughtful too! Over the years he expressed his thoughtfulness toward Sally, time and time again.

However, she really noticed it that very day when he leaned in and whispered to her, "I know if your mom were still alive, she would've been so very proud of you too!"

You see, Sally's mother died a year earlier when she was a junior, after being on Gentle Shepherd Hospice for several months. During that time, Ben and Sally's friendship seemed to have no other option but to grow into love—a mutual love that made those two inseparables during their senior year at Madison High, sort of like peaches and cream, like bread and butter, like cold and winter, and like peanut butter and jelly (you get the picture).

They graduated in May and married in June, on the fifteenth. Theirs was a small church wedding with a lawn reception on the farm that followed. The mixed-and-matched picnic tables were covered with soft-yellow tablecloths. Their centerpieces were quart mason canning jars, overflowing with yellow wildflowers, wildflowers that her mother had planted in their corner flower bed, next to the oldest oak tree on the farm. And as for Sally, their presence there felt like her momma was sharing in on her important day.

Ten months later, it was spring. Ben was so enthusiastic regarding his plans for the new corn crop that he had just planted. Happier was he in fulfilling the promise he had made to Sally's father right before his passing. That promise was to keep Bethesda Acres farm going, and it was a promise that Ben Rogers planned on keeping—even though in keeping it, Ben knew that it would mean a lot of hard work and a lot of sacrificing by both him and Sally!

Over the years, Ben and Sally had witnessed firsthand several area farms in Harrison County that had to liquidate, leaving them, having to say goodbye to a few childhood friends. The only advantage Ben and Sally had over them was that they didn't have a lien on their farm—thanks solely to Homer and Mary Anne Glick, Sally's parents frugal lifestyle. Their chosen way of life enabled Ben and Sally's debt-free beginning, and that was something they both say they were eternally grateful for.

Recently, Ben had to say goodbye to his closest neighbor, Joe Sturm. Joe's cattle farm, Whispering Oaks, was sold at an auction, forcing him to move his family to Peoria, Texas, where there he found work on his brother-in-law's spread.

Joe sold all his farming equipment and livestock too. However, he could not bring himself to sell his children's 4-H project, Little Lester, to a stranger. Little Lester was a miniature horse, and for whatever reason, one of Joe's beagle pups, named Champ, became his shadow. That lop-eared pup would follow Little Lester from daylight till dark. Wherever Little Lester went, Champ was not far behind! Put them both together, and that team made up the best security system a landowner could ever wish for. Running to the farm's entrance gate, whinnying and barking, they would alert Joe every time someone would pull onto the Whispering Oaks gravel drive.

Sad to say, because of the reality of the situation, there was no place for a miniature horse and a beagle pup on a busy cattle operation in the heart of Texas. This left Joe having to explain why they could not move them to Texas with his two young daughters. The girls tearfully tried to understand.

"It would be okay to leave them behind, Daddy, if you promise us that you'll find them a good home."

Joe knew, with time being a factor, he quickly needed to find them both that new home!

That's how Bethesda Acres Farm became home to an auburn-colored miniature horse and a brown, white, and mostly black purebred beagle pup. They were gifts from the Joe Sturm family to Ben and Sally Rogers (*mostly Ben*). Sally was so pleased with Ben in welcoming Joe's gift because she had firsthand knowledge that his obligation plate was already full!

It was Ben and Sally's mutual admiration and fondness that they shared towards one another that would ultimately keep them close as they'd walk through three of the greatest heartbreak periods that a young couple should ever have to endure.

"Sally," Ben said, "Jim and Marcy wants to introduce you to their two sons. Keith is twelve years old, and Cody's ten."

Both boys presented themselves as polite youngsters. Both Ben and Sally were looking forward to getting to know the Jones family better as time went by. Hopefully, they'd choose to make Freedom Community Church their place of worship. Coming over, Reverend Palmer joined in on the handshaking, giving the Jones family a warm invitation to return next Sunday, adding the fact that it would also be Communion Sunday service.

As the Jones family left the church building, they all four had smiles on their faces, mixed with the hope that this congregation would become their new church family.

Reverend Palmer turned to Ben with a chuckle, saying, "It won't be hard to keep up with the Jones, since I shop at Mercer's at least once a week. Get it? Keep up with the Jones, ha-ha!"

The three of them stood there exchanging a brief time of laughter. Ben and Sally both seemed to enjoy Reverend Palmer's light comedic side.

Reverend Palmer was new as their pastor. His wisdom showed that he was not new to the pulpit, just new to Madison. Their pastor before him, Reverend A. E. Barnhart, retired and moved to Pensacola, Florida. He was an older man with old ways. Unlike Reverend Palmer, he never included current issues and events with their relevance according to the Word of God concerning their small-town USA.

Another difference was that Reverend Palmer took it upon himself every Sunday to personally hand Ms. Sally her very own copy of that week's church bulletin. (*It always included his sermon notes.*) He did this to keep her informed, and it was his way of letting her know that he valued her faithfulness in serving the preschoolers of his congregation.

He knew that for Freedom Community Church to survive, it needed the next generation to attend and to minister God's goodness to others. That Sunday, the bulletin's cover was adorned with an autumn harvest scene: pumpkins, hay bales, a red wooden wagon, and plenty of colorful fall flowers.

Reverend Palmer had a threefold purpose on locating Ben. First was to have Ben introduce him to the Joneses. Second was to give Sally her bulletin, and the third was that he needed to talk with Ben before he left to go home. Of course, Sally agreed to wait.

She said, "Go on, I don't mind. I'll be in the car catching up on some of my reading," pointing to today's church bulletin she held in her right hand.

Ben and Reverend Palmer made their way to his office.

"Ben, I have great news! But first, how much was the goal you set for the mission's fund-raiser for the Appalachian Youth Center?"

Ben answered, "Our youth group had hoped to raise five hundred dollars."

"Well, I am about to blow you away, son. The grand total that was raised is fourteen hundred dollars!"

Ben, usually a talkative man, kept silent as Reverend Palmer gave out the following details.

"You and our youth group raised seven hundred dollars from the apple sales and the three car washes that the Wells Fargo Bank had sponsored. I believe one was in July and the other two was in August, correct?"

"That's correct."

"This week our Senior Saints group heard how hard the youth group had worked ... That motivated them into unanimously deciding to match the seven hundred dollars raised, making the grand total fourteen hundred dollars!"

Reverend Palmer told Ben that he'd have Melody, the church's treasurer, make out a check in the morning and that he had meetings until noon. He promised Ben that he'd personally get the check out in the afternoon's mail.

"Ben, what are you doing tomorrow?"

Ben replied, "I'm a little behind on my fence repairs that must be done tomorrow. Because Tuesday and Wednesday, I'm needing to clear the back and front cornfield to get ready to plant my winter ground cover. Then, as you well know, Thursday is Thanksgiving, and my Sally likes to take Friday off too! She loves to bargain hunt on Black Friday, and I have the distinct pleasure in going with her to Verona. I think she wants me to tag along, just to carry the shopping bags!"

"Well, I was thinking, you've been so busy with the fund-raiser, I knew you must be a little behind on your chores. So why don't I come over and help you get caught up? How is it that I've never come to your place yet? We both have talked about it, but let's do more than talk this time, what do you say?"

"Pastor, I would like that."

"Ben, I'll be there right after I mail the check. The center's director should have the money by next week. You did a good thing, and I'm very proud of you, son!"

Sally didn't have to wonder for very long why they both had to meet because she was stopped by Melody in the parking lot. Melody told Sally the good news but made her promise that she would let Ben tell her all the details for himself (and that she needed to act surprised!). Again, another situation presented itself that caused Sally to have a sense of pride in her Ben. It was his character of faithfulness that made him stand out in Madison's community as a godly man.

Sally opened her bulletin to read the Scripture of the Day: Psalms 139. Next she read the Pastor's Prayer Suggestion for the Week: "Pray for mothers everywhere." Finally, she read her favorite section entitled: "Did YOU Know?" This week's topic is "Abortion Statistic in the World, Including America."

According to WHO (World Health Organization), every year in the world there are an estimated **40–50 million abortions**. This corresponds to approximately **125,000 abortions** per day. In the USA, where nearly half of pregnancies are unintended and four in 10 of these are terminated by abortion, there are over 3,000 abortions per day.

Go to this site for active counter in live time: http://www.worldometers.info/abortions/.

Throughout the United Sates, there are about 1.3 million abortions each year, which works out to 3,562 abortions each day, according to the *New England Journal of Medicine*.

Usually, the bulletin's "Did YOU Know" section was full of pleasant facts. But these statistics left Sally in a state of sadness.

Ben's meeting was a surprise to him. He got in the car so happy his face was lit up like a Christmas tree!

"Sally, we raised fourteen hundred dollars for the Appalachian Youth Center. Can you believe it!"

Sally was so glad for Ben! However, during the drive home, it was unusually quiet between them.

As for Ben, his joy became unspeakable as his mind wondered about the different scenarios that their gift would bring to the Appalachian youth. Would the money be used to buy a new basketball banking board, hoop, and net; or a few new footballs; or camping equipment; or maybe something practical like a new sink or commode for the girls' bathroom? Better yet, maybe a fun-filled evening at the skate rink, serving as the youth's Christmas party. In all his wondering, Ben seemed not to notice Sally's silence at all.

Sally was so relieved because those abortion statistics had rendered her speechless as well. No words could be spoken that would effectively explain to Ben the depth of sadness she was experiencing.

Each day the loss of 3,562 tiny little ones at the hands of their very own mother's choice. This fact caused Sally's heart to cry out— *not* in judgment, but in an overwhelming concern. Her heart cried, but her eyes concealed her pain from Ben.

Little Lester and Champ met Ben and Sally at the farm's entrance gate. They both acknowledged Ben's two new buddies. After that the noisy team ran over to shade under the weeping willow tree next to the pump house. Hand in hand, Ben and Sally went inside. Once there, as usual, Ben turned on the TV already tuned into the local weather station. This allowed him to get updates and to watch that upcoming week's *"Farm Report."*

On top of their vintage console TV set was Ben's sketch pad and pencil set. During the winter months, with nothing much happening, he'd bring them out and draw subjects that he saw around the farm. After all, the farm was nearly everything to him.

Sally slipped off her dress shoes and put her floral tote on the desk. Next she began to make dinner for two. She was so glad to get busy, hoping that it would take her mind off those disturbing statistics, but not before asking herself, "Is anyone else in the congregation feeling what I am feeling about those 3,562…?"

From the refrigerator, she pulled out a small baked ham trimmed with a brown sugar glaze, whole cloves, pineapple slices, and maraschino cherries. She sliced a loaf of her homemade sourdough bread and some homegrown vine ripened big-boy tomatoes. She opened a jar of sweet pickles then placed Ben's southern pecan pound cake in the center of their dining room table.

His cake was sitting on Sally's great grandmother's crystal cake plate, covered with its matching etched glass dome lid. Iced tea and a bowl of potato salad were also on the table. *Oops!* Sally almost forgot. She jumped up to get the mayo and a knife. Now they were ready for Ben to say grace.

After the blessing, he sliced the prepared ham for their feast to begin. Thirty minutes later, Ben had a full stomach. Once again, he was satisfied with Sally's tasty meal. He kissed her on the top of her head as he went over to the coffee pot to pour them both a fresh cup of coffee to enjoy with dessert. They didn't talk much during their meal. However, it was Ben's dessert conversation that announced a couple of surprises to Sally—the first surprise being that the Joneses told him that both of their sons were once foster children. The boys were brothers, and they adopted them a couple of years ago.

Sally said, "But how can that be? They look like a real family."

Ben replied, "Honey, they are a real family!"

The next was that Reverend Palmer was going to come by tomorrow afternoon to help him repair some fencing.

Surprised, Sally said, "Well, that's a first! Does he even know how to repair a fence?"

Ben said, "I doubt it, but it will be a good time of fellowshipping, and besides, I'll keep a close eye on him!

"Sally, another good meal! Thank you! Since we have so much leftover, let's invite Reverend Palmer to stayover tomorrow for supper to share in our abundance. What do you say?"

Sally agreed that they should, as Ben left to join his two furry friends in walking the land to survey what was next on his workload priority list.

Sally's cleanup was light and easy enough, only taking thirty minutes. She wondered what to do with the rest of her afternoon. She could...? Hearing music coming from the living room, she realized that Ben had once again forgotten to turn off the TV—as one of those louder-than-normal monster truck commercials had given him away again.

She looked toward heaven and said, "That man that you gave me, Lord! He can find the *on* button, but he just can't seem to find the *off* one. How's that possible?" She laughed.

As she went to turn off the TV, the next commercial message captivated her attention.

"Stop abortion now! Are you aware that ..." the announcer said, "according to WHO (World Health Organization), every year in the world there are an estimated *40 to 50 million abortions*. This corresponds to approximately *125,000 abortions* per day. In the USA, where nearly half of pregnancies are unintended and 4 in 10 of these are terminated by abortion, there are over 3,000 abortions per day. Throughout the United Sates, there are about 1.3 million abortions each year, which works out to 3,562 abortions each day, according to the *New England Journal of Medicine*."

Sally spoke out loud, "Lord, there're those abortion statistics again. Those are the same ones Reverend Palmer shared with us in today's bulletin. Is this where he got them from? Three thousand five hundred sixty-two? Really? I knew it must have been a lot, but I had no idea it was that many."

Turning off the TV, she took her now-heavier heart out onto the front porch. There she had hopes of comforting it, by rocking—hopefully to keep it from breaking. After fifteen minutes, she realized that her racing thoughts refused to let her be comforted. Those darn numbers...*24* hours, *1* day, and *3,562* abortions.

During the ride home from church, her crying was silent, but now she was home and her eyes joined in as the tears began to flow.

Later in life, Sally could only describe what she was feeling by saying, "The lyrics in Allison Durham Spears song 'Break This Heart'[1] says it all!"

> Laughter comes through heartache
> Growing comes through pain
> And, Lord, I know you're slowly teaching me
> I have to lose to gain
> I've been all too careful of vessels and of jars
> So won't you let your love break through the walls
> Releasing what you are
> Break this heart, let it be open
> I know it is no good 'til the bitterness is gone
> Make my life a vessel that's broken
> So I can someday help the one who falls
> There's nothing worse than nothing
> To live yet not to feel
> I've been numb to all the suffering
> I've had a heart as cold as steel
> Make me strong and tender, take away my fears
> And give me holy insight, Lord
> And wash my eyes with tears ...
> So I can someday help the one who falls

---

[1] Writers: Ed Fry, Gloria Gaither, and Benji Gaither. Publishers: Townsend & Warbucks Music / ASCAP, Gaither Music Company / ASCAP

As those sorrow-filled tears ran down Sally's cheeks, she cried out to God, "Why? Why do those statistics trouble me so? I've never had an abortion! I don't even know anyone who has! Lord, answer me please…Why me? And while we're at it, tell me something—how could so many mothers just get rid of their unborn babies when all Ben and I ever wanted was to keep the three I couldn't carry?"

Sally left her now-uncomfortable rocker, making her way over to her mom's wildflower bed. There in its center were three tiny white crosses that she and Ben had placed there (one for each of their babies.) Sally refused to say her babies were lost because they were not! *For she knows where they are*!

As she and Ben would put in place each tiny cross, they said the same simple prayer:

"Dear Lord, would you see to it that Grandma Glick could look after her grandbabies until we get there. We know that they would get exceptionally good care and would be given a whole lot of *lovin'* too!"

Maybe to most, that prayer would sound a little simplistic on such a solemn occasion. But for Ben and Sally, it brought the big comfort that they both needed, which allowed them to go on.

Sally pulled a few weeds then looked around at the front field. She noticed it was still full of dried cornstalks needing to be cleared. No worry! She knew Ben would get to it before their first big freeze. Even with her attention being elsewhere, Sally could not escape the 3,562.

Sally recalled Reverend Palmer's prayer request, to pray for mothers everywhere. So she did just that.

After praying, she begins counting cornstalks. One, 2, 3, 20, 21, 22, 40, 42, 75, 76, 105. At 106, she reached the scarecrow that she and Ben had made from an old broom and some straw. They dressed it in Ben's old flannel shirt and a pair of her faded blue jean overalls. To finish their masterpiece, Ben gave it his old soiled straw hat that he was wearing.

They strategically placed an old apple crate beside him so that they would have a place to take their break, drinking a cool glass of water in the heat of their workday.

Sally sat for a moment beside that scarecrow and made sure he knew that he was the least scariest scarecrow that she'd ever seen! She laughed till her toes curled. She also had noticed that there were some blue lavender morning glories that had made their way into Ben's corn crop, climbing up several of his sun-dried cornstalks.

Yes, they were pretty, but they couldn't be allowed to invade Ben's future rows of corn! So she made a mental note to let Ben know of their invasion. Sitting there, Sally also noticed a few of her mother's yellow wildflowers growing. The wind and the birds must have scattered their seeds onto the farm's fertile soil. From there they simply took root. She pulled the wildflowers up by their roots and carried them inside.

Trimming off the roots, she placed them in a quart mason jar then placed the arrangement in the center of the kitchen table and wondered, if Ben would remember them as being the same centerpiece that they had at their wedding reception. Sally put an aspirin in the water as her friend Connie had suggested. They both wanted to try this experiment after reading online that it would keep them fresher longer. Now the experiment was on! Sally planned on giving Connie an update on the results when she talked to her next Sunday.

That centerpiece left Sally desiring to see her wedding photographs. She pulled her unfinished scrapbook from the living room bookshelf. Opening it to the first page, she saw there the photographs of her and Ben as babies. On the second were their wedding photos. Her favorite was the one where they got a little more comfortable, changing into their blue jeans, standing beside a picnic table. On that picnic table was their triple-tiered wedding cake trimmed with blue buttercream frosting. On its top was a bride-and-groom figurine.

She still has that figurine somewhere out in the shed. She froze the cake's top layer as everyone had suggested. Ben and Sally brought it out on their first anniversary and took a bite…horrible-tasting, simply horrible!

Ben asked Sally, "And…why do we need to eat old cake?"

"I think it's for good luck."

Ben answered back, "We'll be lucky if we don't get sick from eating it! I have an idea, let's enjoy a piece of your fudge cake instead!"

So in the trash that top layer went and with it their luck *did not*!

The few pages following were full of photos of their parents and Ben's family. Sally being an only child, the closest thing to a sister she ever had was her favorite aunt, Aunt Wilma, ten years older than she. Her Aunt Wilma and her husband (Uncle Bill) and their children, and now grandchildren, took up four pages. Next was a photo taken at Sally's fourteenth birthday party.

"*Well, looky there!* There's young Ben Rogers wearing his new tractor cap, trying to push me a lot higher than I really wanted to go. After all, it was my new tire swing, and I should be able to swing as high or as low as I wanted to go!"

Next to it were her two blue ribbons, a photo of her family and Ben swimming at Lake Stony, a photo of Ben's first tractor, one of their new corn harvest, and one of their first Thanksgiving turkey with all the trimmings. The very last photo in the scrapbook was a picture of their first Christmas as man and wife. They trimmed their tree in all red bulbs. Sitting beside it was a rocking chair—a gift from Ben, to be used in their baby nursery.

Little did they know then that their three pregnancies would end in three miscarriages, instead of ending happily by them bringing home a precious pink or blue bundle of joy. With Ben and Sally's third miscarriage went all their hopes, dreams, and prayers for children. Sally's heart was deflated. Ben could not bear to see Sally's deepest longing go unfulfilled. So he purposed himself in filling that void—to fill her life with as much happiness that he could possibly cram into her lifetime.

Over the years, they'd survived by living harvest to harvest as Sally reconciled to be content with caring for the toddler preschoolers that God sent her way at Freedom Community Church. And as for that rocker, it was the very same one that she sits on every Sunday, rocking her little ones, giving them the tender, loving, care that they deserve.

Sally heard Ben wiping his feet. She quickly closed the scrapbook, placing it back on the shelf. Ben burst's through the kitchen door! Cradled in his arms were a few granny smith apples, tomatoes, hot banana peppers, and one tiny pumpkin. He looked just like a little boy desiring some praise for the treasures that he had just found. Sally took his bounty, placing them in the sink. Then she gave him that *big* hug he was looking for.

Ben had that wonderful outdoorsy autumn smell on his old Carhartt jacket. His ears felt cool to the touch. That usually was the first sign that cold weather was on its way to Madison.

Sally thanked God for Ben more and more as their time together seemed to fly by. After all, she had finally found herself at a place where she didn't sweat the small stuff that he did—like forgetting to put the toilet seat down, not closing the kitchen cabinet door after getting a drinking glass out of it, not changing his socks until she reminded him to, and now, the latest thing on his list ... forgetting to turn off the TV before he left the room! After all, his easy chair had no need of hearing the farm report now, did it?

"God knows I love that man," she said, thanking God that he was hers and she was his ...

After all, godliness with contentment is great gain. "Isn't that what the Bible says?"

Today's tears were gone now. Tomorrow would be another day. However, there remained one more prayer to be prayed. Looking over at Ben fast asleep, Sally slipped out of bed onto her knees to pray for mothers everywhere.

Then Sally told God, "*Good night.*"

Climbing back into bed, Ben awakened, saying, "Honey, I almost forgot, I need to ask you something. Those yellow flowers on the table are beautiful. Are they the same flowers we had at our wedding?"

They both cuddled and giggled like newlyweds, and that night they behaved like newlyweds too!

...It's noon already! "Where does the time go?"

Sally thought while she turns on the local FM station. On Mondays, they only played the best mix of the '90s. She swayed and sang to Prince's "Little Red Corvette" and Cindy Lauper's "True Colors." She was washing lunch dishes as she heard a knock on her front door.

There stood Reverend Palmer without a suit on! He was wearing what looked like to be brand-new pair of Levi's blue jeans, a new gray flannel shirt, and a new pair of Red Wing boots. On top of his head was a Razorback baseball cap.

"Pastor, is that you?"

"Sure is," he replied.

"Ben's out in the barn. I'll call him on his cellphone to let him know you're here. I probably don't have to because his alarm system is going off!"

Sally pointed to Little Lester whinnying and Champ barking! They both shared in a healthy dose of laughter as she joined him there on the front porch.

Pastor Palmer was in awe, pointing toward a red-tailed hawk flying over the pond. They swung and rocked while waiting on Ben. Sally offered him a glass of sweet iced tea.

He declined the offer, saying, "No thanks, but maybe a little later." He asked Sally, "Do you mind living next to Carol's Place?"

She quickly answered, "No, both Ben and I rather enjoy sitting here on the porch, looking at the different license plates. We wonder where they're going and what's their reason for going. Yesterday evening we saw someone from Colorado, Iowa, Virginia, and as far away as Canada."

"Bethesda Acres Farm, where did that name come from?"

Sally told him that the name came from her parents.

Then he asked, "Do you know what *Bethesda* means?"

"No, I really have never thought about it."

He went on to instruct her that in the Bible, *Bethesda* means "a place of mercy" and that it was an actual place found in John chapter 5 and many were healed there.

Ben popped around the corner of the house with two pair of gloves fit for farmwork!

"Well, you're here! Come on, let's get going! I'll start by introducing you to a couple of my noisy friends. Then we'll hop on the tractor and go to the back forty. Sally, if you need us, that's where we'll be."

Ben then turned back to Reverend Palmer, saying, "It's getting to be a little cooler, here's an old jacket. You should put it on."

Sally addressed Pastor Palmer, "Pastor, before you guys go off to play ... would you please plan on staying for supper."

With a big smile he answered, "I was hoping that you'd ask. Because Gwen [his wife] went out of town to visit a sick classmate. I was planning on making a frozen dinner."

"Well, that settles it…Supper's at seven."

As her squeaky screen door closed, Sally could be overheard saying, "Um, Bethesda, *a place of healing*!"

Chapter Two

Twenty-Five Years Earlier (It Was the '90s!)

CLARION, ALABAMA, IS KNOWN AS "a small town with big smiles."

This morning in Clarion there was a little nip in the air. It was apparent that winter didn't want to surrender its place on the calendar unto spring just quite yet! Stark reality was that it must! Because the first day of spring was only three days away.

Just as the sun peeked through the low-lying clouds, the children in Mrs. Blagg's Sunday school class anxiously awaited their dismissal. They attended Willow Creek Baptist Church (WCBC), smack-dab in the middle of Bristol County, just north of Mobile.

The church's building was midnineteenth-century architecture. It was the focal point in Clarion's historical district. Most of Clarion's citizens had either had family members married there or held funeral services of a loved one there. Its huge fellowship hall was one of the largest meeting places in town. It too had held countless wedding receptions, benefit gatherings, baby dedications, and men's flapjack pancake breakfasts—just to name a few.

The Bristol County Ladies League held its monthly organizational meeting there, the second Tuesday of every month, where it had done so since its inception in 1949. This month's topic of interest was the publishing and sale of the league's annual *Southern Gal's*

Cookbook. The cookbooks profits were used for the continual beautification of Bristol Counties municipal parks.

Clarion's town park was a breathtaking sight to behold and a photographer's dream. Any given day, you could stroll through watching, as models and wedding parties were being photographed for their wedding albums and for well-known publications. A recent photo of it, was seen in a publication across the pond in London, England. Imagine that.

In the park, there were rows of Cypress trees and stately oaks along the stone walkways, all leading to its garden center. At its center there was a bronze statue of football's great "Brad Stark," a native of Alabama. He was also a relative of the Betts family in Clarion (*but more about that family later in this chapter*). Brad himself even attended the statues unveiling ceremony. In his humble speech, he let it be known how honored he was with Clarion's recognition of him and his accomplishments.

Birdbaths, a goldfish pond, wooden benches, rows and rows of annual and perennial flowers—all thanks to the *Southern Gal's Cookbook* sales.

The buzz going around town was that at last week's meeting, the league's residing president, Wanda Ashcroft, announced that this year's cookbook, for the first time, would include two new sections dedicated to healthy snacks and healthy entrees. This was made possible by a 76–1 vote. The only "*nay*" vote came from Mrs. Francis Betts.

Francis Betts was the league's oldest member and a lifelong resident of Clarion. Their family's stately mansion was built by her husband's great-great-grandfather. Baird Betts, her husband of sixty-one years, had recently passed away. He was the president of the Betts Cotton Company. Francis has never been one known to like change, especially if it was not her idea! Other than some high-mindedness and the fact that she resisted any threat to her beloved Southern traditions, Mrs. Betts really was a fine "Southern lady!"

If the walls of the Betts mansion and the grounds on their estate could talk, they would proclaim accolades regarding the Betts family! There they had held countless benefits to aid the victims of natural disasters, hosted homecoming parties for Bristol's servicemen and women that returned home to their beloved Alabama, and all those grand ballroom parties held in honor of dignitaries from across the United States as well as abroad. The Betts family especially loved entertaining politicians—including last year's formal ball honoring the current governor of the great State of Alabama!

(Politicians, I almost forgot to mention them!) Many politicians that had been voted into office was done so at Willow Creek Baptist Church since it was the polling place for the First District. (You get the picture.) You can now see that Willow Creek Church was a very busy place and a vital part of Clarion's Southern way of living.

This week's Sunday service had concluded, and everyone knew to stand clear of the church's side doors! For they were about to fling open! Mrs. Blagg could be overheard instructing her dismissed class to "exit by walking and not to run please!"

First out the double doors were the Swiger twins. They'd hold the doors open for their classmates as they made their way onto the playground. There some students chose to jump rope, toss around a Frisbee, throw the football, slide down the slide, but most enjoyed taking their turn riding the merry-go-round.

Naturally, the teenage girls gathered around the teenage boys, cheering on their efforts with the football as the athletes completed one pass after another. As in most small towns, Clarion had *the* most popular boy.

His name was Corey Tatterson. He was a senior at Clarion High and was in the ROTC training program there. After graduation, he planned on going directly into the Army—something his parents did not encourage but were willing to accept. Corey played catch with his classmates while keeping a watching eye on his little brother and baby sister (just as his mother instructed him too).

His baby sister and her best friend were considered two of the cutest little girls in all of Bristol County. These cuties were Miss Katie Vincent and Miss Mary Elizabeth Tatterson. Mary Elizabeth was known as Sissy—a term of endearment her big brother Corey gave her when she was born and it stuck! As mentioned, the Tatterson's had another son. He was eleven months younger than Sissy. His name was Austin. He loved tagging along with Sissy and Katie. Over and over, Austin let Katie know that he was going to marry her when they grew up! Katie just laughed it off by informing him that she would not be marrying him because she was going to marry her daddy!

Sissy and Katie exit the church by holding hands, skipping their way to the abandoned swing set. Austin followed, pestering them by trying to untie the blue and green ribbons in their hair.

Sissy was the tinier of the two and had curly red hair and azure blue eyes. Her mother chose a soft blue ribbon this morning to tie back her abundance of curls. She was wearing a frilly blue-striped dress with shiny red shoes. Katie was the taller of the two, having long, straight light-brown hair and vivid green eyes. This morning her mother braided her hair, dressed her in pink, and tied a green ribbon at the tip of her braid. That made Katie so very happy because after all, green had always been her favorite color!

Many said Katie's maturity level was far greater than most her own age. They attributed this to being an only child and that she spent most of her time with just adults. It was only a theory, but it might be true.

These two little girls looked so very different. These young friends would have to live a few more years and travel down several miles before it would be revealed how different they really were (as their friendship would be tested a time or two). But for now they'd giggle, have sleepovers and teatimes with peanut butter and jelly sammiches, and share several boxes of cherry Popsicles while watching the sun go down from the stoop of Vincent's front porch.

Today they'd swing as long as they can, hoping the adults would take their time as Pastor James and his wife greeted each member on their way down the church's front concrete stairs.

Pastor Sydney James was a soft-spoken man until he got to the part in his sermons entitled "Decision-Making Time." That was when he talked louder and even louder—as if God himself was saying, "Pay attention! This decision is about choosing heaven or hell, and it's a very important one!"

It was during one of those decision-making times when best friends Katie and Sissy went forward hand in hand, shoulder to shoulder. They wanted to let Pastor James know that they both chose heaven! After hearing this, he reverently prayed with them at the altar. Mrs. James, being nearby, presented them with their very own Bible. It wasn't like the tiny white Gideon's Bible they were used to carrying. No! It's a large one that had both the Old and the New Testaments in it. Pastor James even took out his silver ballpoint pen and signed their names on the front page. He also wrote in his favorite scripture: Proverbs chapter 3, verses 5 and 6. To the members of WCBC, it was no surprise that these two friends would make such an important decision together, because they did everything together and this day was just like all the rest.

When the service concluded, Pastor and Mrs. James spoke with both of their parents concerning Katie and Sissy being water-baptized next month. This baptismal service would be held at the home of none other than Mrs. Francis Betts. It would take place in her swimming pool, with Mrs. Betts hosting a small get-together afterward—small for Francis, considering only a couple hundred people would be in attendance.

Those two close-knit friends had another thing in common: they both loved Mrs. Harriet James.

They said, "Our pastor's wife always smells like homemade bread baking in the oven." Also that "She was just as sweet as the candy she keeps in her pockets!" They knew when they memorized their assigned Bible verses and when they both sat quietly while her husband preached, she would reward them from those sweet pockets!

Mrs. James's gray hair was long. However, they didn't know how long it was because she always kept it up in a neatly styled bun. Her cheeks were puffy, soft, and rosy. Sissy was amazed with all the freckles that Mrs. James had on her arms and on her hands.

"That must be the reason why they're so warm and why she gives the best hugs in town!" Also, she was the only grandma in Clarion that both Sissy and Katie knew that giggled like they did!

After Sunday service, Katie and Sissy would swing until they'd hear their mom or their dad call out their names. Then they'd pump their legs one last time and jump to the ground running as fast as their legs could carry them toward the church's parking lot. Because they both knew what was next ... *Sunday dinner.*

Most vehicles parked in the church's parking lot were station wagons and vans, mainly because most families that attend WCBC had a lot of kids. For example, the Pearsons had five, the Yopps had seven, the Kinnes had six, while Katie's family only consisted of three...Katie, her mom, and her dad.

Katie's dad couldn't drive her mom's car to church because the back seat was always full of boxes and more boxes. Her mom hosted kitchen-supply parties (part-time) and used her car as both her office and a supply room—leaving the Vincent's mode of transportation to be her dad's old blue Ford pickup. That was okay with Katie because the only other alternative would be coming to church in her dad's vintage Volkswagen Super Beetle. It was ugly and sure needed a lot of work! And now it needed a new engine. Katie overheard her dad telling her grandpa that "it threw a rod" (whatever that meant).

Katie's dad opened his door to help her mom in. She slid to the middle, giving Katie the window seat. That was splendid for Katie because she was able to window-shop the downtown Clarion stores (especially during Christmas.) Katie counted the days until Gabe's Department Store would be putting up their window displays... packed full of toys and other goodies. Then she'd carefully consider all her choices before writing her wish list letter to Santa, in hopes that his elves could make the exact toys she had chosen.

Katie's careful viewing of Gabe's storefront was only made possible because the traffic light that was directly in front of his place of business was the longest red light in town. It stayed red just long enough for all of Clarion's boys and girls to choose what they wanted for Christmas!

Gabe was a very busy man. He owned the store, and he was also the mayor of Clarion.

Katie overheard her mom once asking her dad if Gabe being the mayor had anything to do with that long light in front of his store. He didn't respond. But they both sure did laugh a lot as he drove away once the red light turned green again!

Their drive home from church was a quick one—just long enough to drive by Pete's Grocery, Walt's Gas Station, Tatterson's Lumber Company (Sissy's father and grandpa's business), Grandpa and Grandma Cain's house, Aunt Mart and Uncle Ralph's boarding house, then finally, passing by Katie's favorite … Mr. and Mrs. Rice's Dairy Freeze.

There, for only a quarter, you could buy a vanilla and chocolate swirl cone. In the summer, Mrs. Rice made her homemade raspberry too! All this goodness for just twenty-five cents. But not today; it was Sunday, and the Freeze was closed. The Rice's went to church too, but not at WCBC. They attended a full gospel church on Swisher Hill Road.

From experience, Katie knew not to ask her parents to stop, even if the Dairy Freeze would've been open, because her mom would just say "No…it will spoil your dinner." (*What does that mean anyway?*)

After traveling over the West Ford River bridge and up to the top of the hill, the Vincents' driveway was on the right. They were now home!

All day long, little Miss Katie had been running. She ran to the breakfast table to eat her oatmeal and toast with Smucker's strawberry jam. She ran to the truck as her dad was reminding her that he didn't like walking into church services tardy. And now she was running upstairs to change into her playclothes—hopefully having a chance to play with her baby doll before supper would be ready.

Just like every other little girl in America, Katie had a favorite baby doll. And just like she and Sissy were best friends, their dolls were too! Sissy named hers Avery. Katie named hers Emmalea. Katie got Emmalea when she was five years old, after seeing her in Gabe's window display four Christmas's ago. It was love at first sight, and she just had to have her.

Later that night, Katie wrote to Santa, describing her in detail. The next day her momma mailed that carefully written letter to Santa's workshop in the North Pole.

Every bedtime for a month, Katie would pray that Santa would put her under their Christmas tree. Christmas morning came, and her prayer was answered! There she was, in a box with a see-through window in front. She had long, curly blond hair, with a bright-red ribbon in it. She wore a red-and-white polka-dot dress, white lace-ruffled socks, and black velvet shoes. Emmalea's best feature was her eyes. They were green just like Katie's. They'd open and close as she moved. Each night Katie would lay Emmalea beside of her and her eyes would close. Then her dad would read to them both from Katie's favorite book, *The Velveteen Rabbit*, before saying their bedtime prayer.

After four years of being Emmalea's mother, just like the Velveteen Rabbit, *Emmalea*, too, looked loved on! Her hair was shorter and had very little curl left. In kindergarten, Katie took her safety scissors, giving both herself and Emmalea a stylish haircut, complete with shorter-than-normal bangs! Also, when new, Emmalea's eyes would open and close, but now her left eye had a permanent wink.

She now wore a homemade light-green flowered dress that her Grandma Wilson made for her. It was made from a scrap piece of quilting material leftover from Katie's cousin's baby quilt. Emmalea went barefooted because she lost her socks and shoes. Katie thought they were misplaced when she took Emmalea and Sissy took Avery to Sissy's Grandpa Tatterson's lake house. There the four of them went for an afternoon swim. Katie was not upset with their loss because she carried Emmalea everywhere she needed to go anyway!

Her purple princess teapot was full of rosewood tea. The table was set. The girls (Katie and Emmalea) had a lot to talk about. Katie also could be overheard teaching Emmalea her nine-year-old version of Mrs. Blagg's Sunday school lesson. The main teatime topic was to plan this week's shopping trip with Sissy and Avery. They were needing to shop for new bathing suits because the last year's didn't fit anymore.

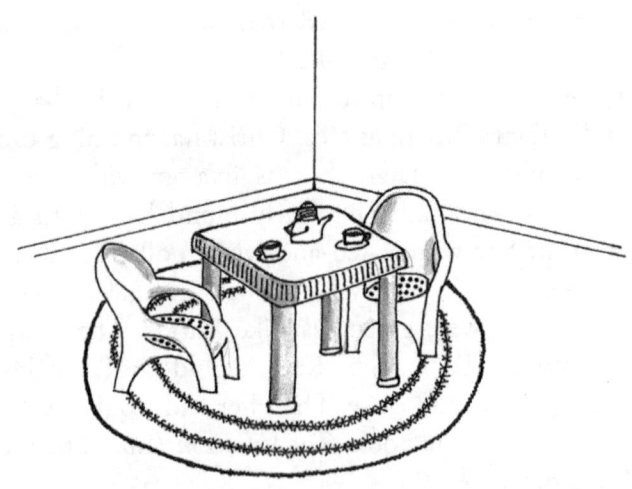

They had just finished eating their make-believe vanilla cupcakes with pink cherry frosting topped with chocolate sprinkles when Katie's mom popped her head in the door, asking, "Are you two having a good time?"

"That's strange…Usually Mom would yell up from the bottom of the stairs, telling me when supper was ready! But not today." Katie wondered, "What's up?"

"Sweetie, I have something special just for you!"

Katie didn't even have time to ask what it was when her mom unfolded her hand, revealing a tiny gold cross necklace.

She said, "My mother gave it to me, and now it's time for me to give it to you."

Katie's mom then opened the clasp and put it around her tiny neck, instructing her, "It's yours, and one day you can give it to your little girl. I waited till now to give it to you because I believe you're old enough to take good care of it."

Katie was so happy!

A special gift just for me! It's not even my birthday or Christmas or anything! she gleefully thought.

She jumped up and ran over to the mirror to see what she looked like with it on. Then Katie turned to show it off to her Emmalea.

"Come on, you two, let's go eat. I made one of your favorites… spaghetti and meatballs."

Chapter Three

Young, Having Fun, Growing Up along the Way!

"Mom," Katie said, "I've been thinking, since I'm thirteen now, I think I'm a little too old to be playing with baby dolls. What do you think?"

"Now, Katie, does Sissy have anything to do with this?"

"Oh no, Mom, she hasn't played with Avery in a long time. Sissy donated her when we donated our brown sofa and those two orange-and-yellow-flowered chairs to the church's yard sale. Remember the one that we had for Pleasant Ridge Horse Rescue Project?"

"Well, come to think of it, I was fourteen, around your age, when my mom, your grandmother, and I wrapped my Suzy Q in her soft-pink baby blanket and put her in the small cedar chest at the bottom of my parents' bed. I still have that old chest up in the attic. Do you want to go up there on Saturday and put your Emmalea with my Suzy Q?"

"You mean, you still have your old baby doll?"

"I sure do! I'll introduce you two to her if you'd like. During lunch we can ask dad if he'll go up to the attic sometime tomorrow or Friday and move a few boxes of Christmas decorations, that box of old dress patterns and a few totes full of yarn and material. Then, I believe we can get to my old chest without any problem."

"Okay, Mom, by then Emmalea and I should be ready."

Her mom lovingly replied, "Now, if you should change your mind, I'll understand. You can just let me know sometime Saturday morning. It sure is nice having some girl time to talk things over, isn't it? Let's go serve up some lunch. You can put the bread and butter on the table. Then you can hand me the soup bowls, and I'll ladle in the cheesy potato soup. While I'm pouring the milk, you can go to the door and call your dad in from the garage. Tell him lunch is ready, he'll come running! I know he must be getting a little hungry by now because he got up early, grabbed a quick cup of coffee and a handful of cookies, then off he went to the garage. I haven't heard from him since."

Saturday came quickly.

"Thanks, honey, for moving all that stuff, making the way clear for Katie and me to get over to that old cedar chest of mine."

"No problem. While you two are doing whatever you're going to be doing, I'm going to make a run into Stalnaker's Foreign Auto Parts Store. Do you girls need anything from town?"

"Dad, we need some milk."

"Honey, if you want, you can pick up some strawberry ice cream from the Dairy Freeze for tonight's dessert."

"Ooh, that's sounds good! I'll be back, it shouldn't take me long."

Katie's dad pulled out of the driveway as she and her mom made their way up the steep attic steps. Katie held Emmalea tightly secured in her arms.

"There she is, I have her. Suzy Q is wrapped in that same pink blanket, just like the day I laid her there."

Katie's mom unwrapped her. Suzy Q was a little frailer than she had remembered. Even one of her legs had popped off.

Katie said, "That's okay, Mom. I have experience with this kinda thing. I can fix it!" So she did.

Gently her mom rewrapped Suzy Q while Katie wrapped Emmalea in a blue afghan that her mom had handed to her. It was one that had been neatly folded in that same chest.

"I want to tell you about that blue afghan. It belonged to my great-great-grandmother, your great-great-great-grandmother! She brought it all the way from Spain to America a very long time ago. She had worn it around her shoulders on the boat to Ellis Island. Remember the story Gramma told us about her traveling to America to become an American citizen?"

Katie teared up as she gave Emmalea one last kiss and one last hug.

Together they laid their babies side by side, on top of a bed made of old black-and-white photographs. Then sadly, they closed the lid.

"Katie, do you smell that? I'm amazed that after all these years, it still smells like a freshly cut cedar tree."

"Mom, you know how I fixed Suzy Q's leg? It's just like what Nurse Margie does to us when she helps Doc Conner. You know, like the time you took me there to get my broken toe fixed. Isn't it?"

"Yes, it's sorta like that, why do you ask?"

"I think I want to be a nurse when I grow up."

"Katie, to become a nurse, you'll have to make really good grades."

"Mom, I know. I will!"

"I have a good idea, the next time we go to Dr. Conner's office, you should share your plans with Nurse Margie. I believe she'll give you some good advice. As a matter of fact, I know she will."

For Margie would be getting a call later that day from Katie's mom, telling her all about their attic conversation.

"Mom, wait, I have to get something!"

"What is it, Katie?"

"My cross necklace! It was getting too tight around my neck so I put it on Emmalea."

"Well, go ahead and get it, I'll wait!"

"Better yet, while you're doing that, I'll look for my high school records and my old record player. I know they're up here somewhere."

"I found them!" her mom said.

"I got it!" Katie said.

"Katie, give me your necklace, I'll put it in my pocket for safe-keeping. I need you to help me with this box please. Look, I must have kept at least twenty records."

They carefully made it down the attic stairs and through its narrow doorway.

Her mom locked the door behind them, saying, "We'll have to buy you a longer gold chain next week when we're in town shopping for Sissy's birthday present."

"Come on, you slowpoke!" Katie yelled at Sissy.

Sissy told Katie that she was running much too fast and needed to slow down! (Anyway, they couldn't catch any fireflies at that speed.)

"We are running faster than they're flying, silly girl, just slow down," Sissy whined.

Sissy's mother had punched a few airholes in the top of an old mayonnaise jar lid and gave it to the girls. Their plan was to catch some lightning bugs and put the jar in their tent as a natural night-light.

It's Sissy's thirteenth birthday. All she wanted was for Katie to sleep over in her family's tent in their backyard, plus a pepperoni pizza from A's Pizzeria, plus chocolate cupcakes with sprinkles on top from Aunt Eldee's Pastry Shop, and of course, her mother's grape Kool-Aid. Mr. Tatterson put up the tent that morning before going to work at their family's lumberyard. After work, he stopped by to pick up Katie at her house. Then together they would stop and get the pizza and the birthday girl's cupcakes!

Earlier in the day, Katie's mom took her shopping to pick out Sissy's birthday gift at Feaster's Jewelry Store. Katie chose a pair of dolphin earrings, since dolphins were Sissy's new favorite thing! They also purchased a longer gold chain for Katie's cross. In the car, her mom reattached the cross to her new longer chain. Katie could hardly wait to wear it and show it off to Sissy, again.

Those two best friends only caught one firefly. Katie had to reach into her hello Kitty backpack to get the pink flashlight out that her mom had packed as a backup plan. Now that they both were thirteen, they did what teenagers do at a birthday sleepover? They stayed up all night, that was what teenagers do! They talked about boys, clothes, planning their weddings, having babies, plans of going off to college together, and becoming nurses just like Nurse Margie.

Also that night they decided to ask Katie's mom to help them win this year's school talent contest. Since Katie's mom brought down her music from the attic, both Katie and Sissy had loved how it made them want to dance, just like she did (ole timey and all!).

Katie would sit halfway up the stairs, peeping through the railing. She'd watch her mom sing into a wooden spoon and dance like she was a teenager again. Once she even saw her dad come in from the garage with his greasy overalls still on. He grabbed her mom, and they slow-danced to a guy singing a nice love song. He then gave her a kiss, grabbed an apple from the fruit bowl, and went back outside, whistling. Katie ran over to see what song was playing. It was "Oh! Carol" on a Tuneware record album. It was sung by Neal Sadaka. It was a memory etched in her mind. She often said it was a memory that she never ever wanted to forget!

Sissy's sleepover went uneventful until the girls heard a noise outside their tent. They unzipped it as quietly as they possibly could to investigate, just as if they both were Nancy Drew. With a full moon staring them in the face, out jumped Austin, yelling, "Boo, I got you!" The girls chased after him. Then he turned around, making a growling sound ... pretending to be Bigfoot! The girls threw the empty pizza box and their shoes at him while begging him to go back inside!

"We're girls, you're just a stinky boy! This is a no-boys-allowed party, Austin Tatterson!"

"Austin, I'll yell for Dad if you don't leave!"

Just then the Tattersons' front porch light came on. Awful Austin ran for the back door.

"I hope he gets in trouble for scaring us like that," Katie said.

Sissy knew he would … if she had anything to do with it!

Summer ended, and a new school year began. The talent show was less than a month away. Sissy and Katie were a bit nervous as they watched their competition practice their talents. Some were singing, some played the guitar, and one classmate even played a violin solo. One talent was puppetry, and Douglas Williams even recited a poem by Charles Dickens that he had memorized.

Since the girls had practiced off and on all summer long, they felt confident and could see themselves winning the Clarion Junior High's first-place trophy. Their talent was to sing and dance to one of Katie's mom's songs, by Nancy Sinatra, entitled, "These Boots Are Made for Walking." Katie's mom and grandma even made them both "go-go" dresses to wear. Sissy's mother did her part by finding them both a pair of white "go-go" boots at a vintage store in Mobile.

Their moms even took them to Mildred's Beauty Salon, having their hair teased and puffed up at the top. Then Mildred tied it with a bright-yellow ribbon. They looked just like Sissy's mother's black-and-white picture of Sandra Dee. (Later in life, what the girls remembered most was all the coughing they did that day when Mildred sprayed their hair with that nasty-smelling Aqua-net hairspray!)

Kimmy Furuso, Jill Anderson, and Debbie Duker won first place. They dressed up like nuns singing a song from the *Sound of Music* while Debbie's brother David played his acoustic guitar. The "go-go girls" came in third.

After the contest, the judges each told Sissy and Katie that they had so much fun watching them dance their routine. It took them back to the good ole days. Katie and Sissy danced moves like, the jerk and the swim.

One judge even said, "I was singing along with you! Could you hear me?" asking them both if they knew that Nancy was Frank

Sinatra's daughter and saying also that they used to dance like that at their high school sock hops.

The lead judge even told Sissy that she had a pair of go-go boots just like hers, until she recently sold them at a consignment store in Mobile. (Sissy looked over at Katie, and they both snickered a little.)

It was the best afternoon the girls ever spent with their moms! They even treated them to a hot fudge ice cream sundae at the Freeze before going home to change.

"Mom," Katie asked, "Who's Frank Sinatra?"

Change.

Change was something both of their mothers had to go through years ago. And now it was Katie's and Sissy's turn. That change was what both girls' lives would be consumed with over the next several years. Both would have to become more focused on their grades. Katie would start working part-time at the Dairy Freeze. She also would have to learn how to save money instead of spending it as fast as she could make it. Sissy needed to learn to become less selfish than she was accustomed to!

Katie also would learn the hard way to come home before dark. One night, after being twenty minutes late, she had been grounded for an entire month. She vowed never to do that again, because it was just not worth it! She'd learn how to make spaghetti and meatballs by following her mom's recipe. (Even her dad would say that he couldn't tell the difference between her mom's meatballs and hers.)

Katie continued to run everywhere she went. However, she would take part in a new form of running when she ran for freshman class president and won. While in office, she started a Clarion High tradition, taking place on the first Saturday in December. The freshman class would meet at six o'clock at the high school's football field parking lot. Students having trucks would stop by Morrison's Seed and Feed Store, and old man Morrison would donate hay to fill the back of their pickups.

The freshman class would pile into their classmates' truck beds, going street to street, house to house, and business to business singing Christmas carols. They'd spread peace on earth and goodwill toward *all* men.

Mrs. Rice would put on a big pot of her special hot chocolate. After the class would sing their last carol to her, "We Wish You a Merry Christmas," she would treat each caroler to a special mug of that hot chocolate—of course, with marshmallows floating on top.

This tradition the Clarion High freshman class upholds, even unto this very day.

That Christmas Sissy and Katie started collecting snow globes, exchanging them as gifts to one another. Also that same year was when Katie's favorite holiday snack changed from rice-crispy treats shaped like Christmas trees to cherry chocolate chip cookies served up with a cup of black coffee, just like her dad took it.

At the age of self-discovery, Katie learned a lot about herself, amazed that she didn't even get upset when she tried out for the JV cheerleading squad and didn't make it. Her dad told her that it was a sure sign that she was maturing into a fine young lady.

Maybe so, Katie thought, *but it might simply have been relief!*

There was only so much time in a day! For both she and Sissy had become a lot more active in their church's youth group, volunteering as assistants to WCBC's youth director, Tim Slagle, and his wife, Bonnie.

Also both girls were busy with the organization of WCBC's holiday gift baskets, which included them being responsible for delivering the baskets to all of Clarion's shut-ins. Using Katie's dad's pickup, they'd shop for food items and fill it with donated food necessities, as well as nonessentials like fruitcakes, mincemeat pies, and bags after bags of hard candies. It appeared senior citizens liked that sort of stuff.

"Yuk, double yuk!" the girls said while making nasty-looking faces!

When delivering the baskets, Sissy and Katie would often be invited to stay and have a piece of fruitcake or a slice of mincemeat pie.

Quickly they'd decline all offers by saying, "No, thank you! We're still full after eating our suppers!" knowing full well that they were both so hungry that they could hardly wait to go through the drive-through for a Whopper and some fries.

Katie was also committed, thanks to her grandfather, in assisting Reverend James in obtaining all updated information on the entire WCBC's membership roster. Then Sissy would enter the data into the church's new computer system. She was doing this labor of love solely because Katie nominated her for the job (against her will).

One of their biggest changes took place the summer of their sophomore year. Instead of being the carefree kids going off to church camp, they were now the coveted activity assistants at WCBC's youth camp for ages nine to twelve. These two friends would run from activity to activity, and yes (just in case you were wondering), Katie had to drag Sissy every step of the way.

Sissy said, "I'd much rather be floating on a raft in my swimming pool, thank you very much, Ms. Katie Vincent! But if you're going to be little Miss Do-Gooder, I guess I will too...After all, it will look good on my college application. Right! Right?"

As part of an activity assistants' duties, they too were obligated to be dorm leaders as well! After instructing the girls to dress for bed and not to forget to brush their teeth, they would all join hands for a group bedtime prayer. Then lights went out promptly at 10:00 p.m. each night. The group then was up at 5:45 a.m., going to breakfast promptly at 7:00 a.m.—that is if they wanted to eat a warm breakfast at the camps mess hall.

On the fourth day of camp, Katie and Sissy reminisced over how much fun they used to have playing those silly camp games—like pin the tail on the donkey, breaking the piñatas, tug of war, and red rover–red rover. After recruiting Austin this year, he too got involved! Under their supervision, he helped organize some of those silly outdoor games like horseshoes, tug of war, volleyball, and sack races—doing his Christian duty only after Sissy and Katie had to promise him something! *(More on that promise later in this chapter.)*

Rev. and Mrs. James watched closely as their camp volunteers donated their time. WCBC's youth camp was a weeklong adventure full of hard work at play! Reverend James decided to reward the group with a few hours of free-time fun. This reward would take place on the last night of camp. Arrangements were made for the campers to be secure in their cabins then to be chaperoned by adult volunteers from the church.

The Jameses' reward was an old-fashioned hayride concluding with a bonfire. The volunteers had hot dogs and roasted marshmallows for making s'mores. They too made several new friendships as well. Happy were they that camp was a success, yet tired from all the long hours in the Alabama sun. The average degree that week was ninety! Sunblock, frequent water breaks, water balloon fights, and several activities in the lake, made it tolerable! Most were surprised at how sad they'd become now that camp was almost over (even Sissy). This was their final activity, to sit around the campfire, singing traditional campfire songs as Randy Garrett played his acoustic guitar. Before calling it a night, many exchanged phone numbers and e-mail addresses.

That was when the weirdest thing happened to Katie Vincent.

Austin leaned in and gave her a kiss, a kiss on her cheek, and told her, "Good night, Katie!"

His kiss made her feel uneasy, to say the least! He had never done that before!

As Katie and Sissy walked back to their cabins, Katie took advantage of the opportunity to tell her best friend what her baby brother had done.

Sissy quickly dismissed it by saying, "It was nothing! Austin didn't mean anything by it! Why, he's like your little brother too!"

Reluctantly, Katie went along with her answer but made it a point to discourage anything like that from happening in the future.

As summer was quickly coming to an end, the girls still had three important dates circled in red on their matching kitty-cat calendars. First, as promised, or as the girls were blackmailed (it just depends on how you look at it), Sissy and Katie needed to teach Austin how to drive. (After all, he so graciously helped them at church camp. Ha!)

Last year, Katie's dad taught her how to drive a stick shift in his old pickup and how to drive an automatic in her mom's embarrassing Subaru (aka the storage shed on wheels.)

Sissy's mother said, "You girls can use my Volvo to teach Austin how to drive in, since we're much too busy with inventory at the lumberyard to teach him."

Katie said, "Thank God, it's automatic."

Even though Katie knew how to drive a standard vehicle, it didn't mean that she wanted to teach Austin how to drive one. Then she overheard Austin asking his dad for the keys to one of their company trucks.

He quickly replied, "No, sir."

That *no* sounded *sooo* sweet to Katie's ears!

Before Mrs. Tatterson handed over her keys to the car, she said, "Come here, you three!" (pointing to the dent that Sissy had put in the bumper of her new car). "I was told that this happened when Sissy hit the trash can at the Chick-fil-A drive-through in Mobile. *That* dent is the only dent I want to see in my new car…got it?"

In unison those three answered, "Yes, ma'am, we got it! We'll be careful."

Austin buckled his seat belt, with the Alabama State testing officer in the passenger's front seat. He started the engine as directed. He placed the car into reverse then backed out of his parking place. He headed toward the stop sign to go out onto the main road. After making three consecutive turns to the right, he found himself at his designated parallel parking spot.

He had practiced parallel parking several times with Katie and Sissy, so his confidence was high that he could accomplish this task without any problem. After parking perfectly, the officer instructed Austin to pull out onto the main drive and head back to the starting point, which he did.

After stopping and turning off the car, the officer said, "That was quite impressive, but answer me one question. What does that sign down there say, where you made your first turn?"

Austin answered, "Stop."

"Did you stop?"

Nervously, Austin answered, "I…I think so?"

"Well, son, you did what we call a rolling stop. You almost came to a complete stop, but instead, the forward motion of the car lasted long enough to disqualify it as being a valid stop. For this reason, you'll have to come back next week and do it all over again. I'm sure you'll not make the same mistake twice."

"No, sir, I'll make a complete stop next week!"

"Good man!" The officer shook Austin's hand, handing him his form that had the *failed* box checked with a big *red* checkmark.

Katie and Sissy couldn't believe that Austin had made such a stupid mistake! Regardless, they both continued to work with him every afternoon so that they could be released from their obligation in holding his hand until he got his driver's license. The following week could not have gotten there quick enough because everyone at Clarion High had heard about Austin's failed attempt (Sissy and her big mouth!). Thanks to her, Austin was teased by his fellow students.

Some were saying, "That's what you get when you have two girls teaching you how to drive, Austin!"

The very same officer was assigned to him again. For the second time, Austin started the car's engine. He stopped the car at the end of his driving test, and the officer told him that he couldn't have done it better himself.

"Thank you, sir, I needed to hear that!"

And with that, Austin was handed his paperwork with a big *red* checkmark beside the word *passed*.

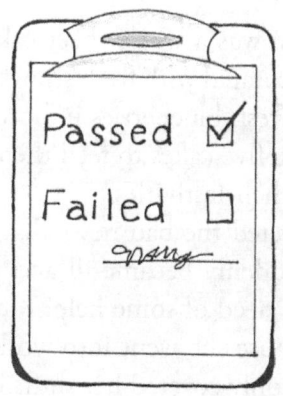

Katie was so proud to tell his mother what a good student Austin had been.

"Austin, you're awesome!" both Katie and Sissy said in congratulating him.

Then the dig came.

"Little brother, even though it did take you two times to pass! I—your much older, much wiser sister—passed mine on the very first try! Sorry, bro, I just couldn't resist the temptation!"

Despite Sissy's snide remark, Austin did feel awesome!

The first thing he wanted to do was to drive to the Tatterson family's grave plot to place a new American flag on his big brother Corey's grave. Corey was buried in Clarion's only cemetery (dating back to the pre-Civil War era).

First event over and done with!

The *second* event took place during the Labor Day weekend. It was the Vincent's annual Labor Day barbeque. It's a weekend full of fun and games, with plenty of food cooked on the grill/BBQ pit. The event's grand finale was a massive firework display. Katie's mom always baked the crowd's favorite dessert, her patriotic cake. It had been a hit every year, and every year Aunt Eldee, of Aunt Eldee's Pastry Shop, tried to persuade her in giving her the recipe! But Mrs. Vincent refused to give it to her year after year.

(If you, the reader, promise not to give the recipe to Aunt Eldee when you see her, Katie's mom will give it to you! It's conveniently located in the back of this book.)

Her patriotic cake was a white sheet cake, with a fluffy white frosting. Its top was decorated with fresh strawberries as the American flag's stripes and with fresh blueberries indicating its stars. This year she planned on making five cakes to feed the hungry Clarion crowd that would join in on their festivities.

No one had expected the bad news that came to Clarion that weekend. Mr. Rice suddenly became ill and passed away. This sad event left Mrs. Rice in need of some help! Katie missed most of the weekend activities because she went into work to cover for her boss (Mrs. Rice). Katie not only covered her shifts but opened and closed the Freeze as well and reordered all supplies that were needed to keep the doors open.

Mrs. Rice was so grateful for Katie because the Dairy Freeze was the Rice's only source of income. And now more than ever, its income was crucial to her financial well-being. The dilemma Katie faced was that she'd not only miss most the barbeque, she'd also have to miss Sissy's seventeenth birthday party (the *third and final* planned event of their summer).

Sissy's birthday party was being held at her Grandfather Tatterson's Smoky Mountain Lake house. It would be the last one that she'd ever have there, since it was under contract and appeared to be sold. If all went as planned, in thirty days, the keys would go to Mr. Howard Toth, principal of Victory High School, and his family.

Instead of Sissy understanding why Katie had no other choice than to do the right thing, she became furious, calling Katie and leaving her several mean-spirited messages. Her friend, with all her pleading, could not sway Katie from keeping her word to Mrs. Rice—even though it meant that she would tick off her best friend of seventeen years.

The whole town knew how spoiled Sissy was! They often wondered how she would react if she was ever told no and how she would react if she didn't get her way! She had always been her daddy's little girl, and whatever Sissy wanted, Sissy got!

Well, that was the case—until now!

On the other side of that friendship was Katie. During her formative years, she was surrounded by good examples, like her grandmother, grandpa, her mom, her dad, and the Rice's too. Because of their positive influences, she would make it through the days and months that Sissy chose to snub her. Katie was deeply hurt by her best friend's insensitivity but refused to retaliate. Instead, Katie prayed a lot, considering the more serious issues of life, like the future.

Katie had heard from another friend at youth group that some boys from Lumberport came to Sissy's party on their Seadoos and that they had brought a cooler full of beer.

Kaye-Kaye also told her, "I've seen Sissy driving through town with a strange boy. I think he's from Lumberport. They were playing loud music and smoking cigarettes. I think they were cigarettes?"

Sissy had also been in a lot of trouble with the principal at school for skipping classes.

Sissy would pass Katie in the hallway and choose not to make any eye contact with her. In this kind of relationship, Katie had no experience to draw from. All she knew to do was to continue praying and to continue sending Sissy e-mails, just as if they were talking as friends face-to-face. Sadly, no responses ever came.

Katie stopped Austin in the hallway, giving him things to give to Sissy—like a Valentine Card, Easter Card, an invitation to her birthday party, and an invitation to her graduation dinner that the Vincent's were hosting. Still no reply from Sissy.

On a positive note…Katie received a lot of good news during Sissy's absence. Even though she was unable to celebrate them with her best friend, Katie still celebrated them with a couple friends at church and with her family, of course. Her family had always been her constant in her life. They were always around and could be counted on as dependable. They especially celebrated Katie when she received the news that she'd been accepted into ISU's nursing program next fall.

(Katie found herself needing a *second opinion* about something.)

She knew that her mom and dad would be truthful regarding an idea she had for increasing Mrs. Rice's profits. As the three of them sat around the kitchen table enjoying a cup of coffee together, Katie introduced her delicious, profit-making idea to them on one of her grandmother's English rose china plates.

"Honey," Dad said, "these are absolutely delicious! Now, what do you want to talk about?"

"Well, I've been thinking about giving Mrs. Rice the recipe for those lemon brownies that you're enjoying. I did the math, and if the Freeze would feature them on Fridays only, Mrs. Rice could make an extra two to three hundred dollars a week. With her increase, she could do some much-needed repairs to her building."

They both encouraged Katie to do just that!

Her mom warned her, however, "Watch out for Aunt Eldee! Wait, come to think of it, this may be a good thing! She might give me a break and hound you every Friday for your recipe instead of my cake recipe!"

"Ha-ha!" Katie laughed as she ran upstairs to sit in front of her computer to modify her recipe from two dozen brownies to ten dozen—something she must do before approaching her boss with her proposal in the morning.

Returning his attention to his brownies, her dad shared his thoughts about Katie with his wife. He felt so privileged in watching their little girl grow up.

"She has changed so gracefully into a fine young lady, one that I had prayed she'd become!"

The Freeze's Friday special was a sweet success! Those lemon morsels brought new life into Mrs. Rice's vision for the Freeze. She was busy planning some repairs and would start them as early as next month.

The senior dance came and went. Katie was dressed in a tea-length lavender dress with matching shoes—ones that her Aunt Mart had bought for her on a shopping trip to Foley. The WCBC's youth group decided that they'd all go together on a group date. And after the dance, the group went to the church's fellowship hall. There the adult Sunday school class hosted a breakfast buffet complete with Belgium waffles and homemade whipped cream.

It was a lot of laughs as Rev. and Mrs. James showed a slide show highlighting the youth group's activities through the years! Nursery photos, kindergarten graduations, vacation Bible school group shots (with most of their front teeth missing), the Fourth of July float-making activities, bake sales, Christmas plays, water-balloon fights and egg tosses at camp, and finally, WCBC's equivalent to the Summer Olympics called "WCBC's Summer Games."

Katie only hoped that no one had noticed her looking over to the room's entranceway. She was hoping to see Sissy walk in. Once again, Sissy disappointed her by not showing up. Katie was now making memories without Sissy in them, a change that left Katie in new territory.

The next day Katie's mom returned from town and said that she ran into Sissy at Walt's while filling up her car with gas. She said that Sissy said "Hi" and that was all she said…

"What's happening with her?"

"Well, Mom, she refuses to answer my calls, my messages, and my cards. She's been isolating herself from our youth group too! She's skipping school, her grades are failing, and when we do run into one another, she avoids me. Kaye-Kaye says that she's even seen her smoking, but she doesn't know what. She's my best friend. What can I do?…Mom, I'm hurting horribly inside!"

Katie began to cry in her mom's arms.

"Oh, sweetie, I don't think all of her actions are just because you were unable to go to her birthday party. Just give her the space she's wanting while you fill yours with something else. As a matter of fact, your father and I think you're doing a pretty good job of keeping busy. Your grandparents say they hardly see you anymore. We understand that with high school classes and homework, working at the Freeze, your activities at church, and you applying for colleges that we too have had to spend less and less time together as a family.

"We realize that soon, we'll be several hundred miles apart, and with this change, we three need to understand that things will never be the same. However, promise me one thing—you'll always keep in touch. We will miss you deeply, because it's always been you, me, and dad. And just because changes happen doesn't mean they'll happen for the worse. After all, doesn't the Bible say something about … all things work for our good, because we love God? You still love God, don't you?"

"Yes, ma'am I do."

"Just like you've had to adjust to Sissy's absence, we too will have to adjust to yours as well. This is a part of growing, and with changes come many benefits and some drawbacks too. Your dad and

I want you to know how very proud we are of you. And through it all, we've noticed that you have never given up on Sissy. Dad and I too will continue praying for her every single day. We have discussed this, and we believe that after she adjusts to all the changes that are happening in her life, she'll come through it just fine!"

Katie dried her eyes then told her, "I love you, Mommy."

Then she fell asleep under her childhood "Precious Moments" quilt that her grandmother made *just for her*!

Chapter Four

Graduation!

June 3ʳᴰ, Katie (known as the Vincent family's only overachiever) was graduating from Clarion High School at two o'clock. Out of this year's senior class of 251, Katie was chosen to be valedictorian. Her parents and Sissy too were remembering all those back-and-forth arguments that the girls had over which one of them would be the valedictorian and which one would be the salutatorian. It was a little sad that it came down to a nonissue because Sissy barely made it.

As if the townsfolk hadn't been gossiping enough about the losses that the Tattersons had suffered, rebellious Sissy was about to give them even more to talk about!

Katie gave a moving valedictorian speech and then handed the podium back over to Vice Principal Carson. He proceeded on to handing out the diplomas. The first was given to Cynthia Alderson, and then the next, and the next, until eventually, it was Sissy's turn.

Popping her bubblegum, as Mr. Carson announced "Ms. Mary Elizabeth Tatterson," she stood and curtsied. As she walked down the aisle toward the stage, she flashed the Clarion's rival school Lumberport's cropped-off football jersey, she was wearing under her gown, at her fellow classmates.

The Lumberport Lumberjacks had been Clarion's Cardinal's bitter rival since their inception.

As if that weren't enough, after Sissy received her diploma and repositioned her tassel from right to left, she shook Mr. Carson's hand then yelled out to the football team, "Losers, losers, you're all a big bunch of losers!"

That was the lowest blow that she could give! Since this year, they had lost the Alabama State Football Championship to the Lumberjacks, 32 to 3.

Katie just hung her head in disbelief, while holding her breath, hoping that Sissy's naughtiness would not cause a riot. Thanks to Mr. Carson's fast thinking, he had dear Reverend James escort Sissy to the back of the auditorium, sitting with her until the ceremony had ended.

Reverend James started attending graduation ceremonies at Clarion High in 1970, and this one would possibly be one *he'd never forget*!

Sissy's parents, Mr. and Mrs. Earnest Tatterson, just sat there stunned. They couldn't say a word. They left speedily when Kevin Zucker's name was called. Leaving with them was their youngest, Austin, but not before Sissy gave him a high five.

Just a little while ago, a rumor had made its way to Katie's ears, saying that Sissy had been hanging out with a couple of Lumberport's football players. Well now, everyone knew that that rumor was, indeed, true and that it was not idle gossip after all.

Today's display did not shock Katie as it did so many others in attendance. Katie always knew that side of Sissy's mischievousness. She also knew the side of Mary Elizabeth Tatterson that was living well below her scholastic potential. Almost all of Sissy's family and friends had talked to her until they were blue in the face. Most had given up on her, but not her best friend, Katie. She absolutely refused too!

Katie's parents insisted that Sissy and her family join the Vincent family in taking post-graduation pictures, taking the opportunity to say, "Sissy, you're always welcome in our home, and Austin too!"

They both were invited again to come over to their home for dinner, but Sissy said, "Nope, I have to run. I made other plans!"

Austin chose to leave with his parents.

Sissy left, walking toward the school's parking lot. There a red Ford Mustang convertible, full of her Lumberport friends, that had been waiting for her.

Katie watched her as she walked away, thinking, *Wait for it, wait for it.*

When halfway to the car, Sissy hesitated and *looked back* at Katie.

There it was! That was the *look* Katie was hoping to see.

That look was one that only Katie could interpret. It was the same *look* they had shared several times before. Like when in the third grade, they were separated by being assigned two different homerooms. That morning, Sissy turned halfway down the hall with that identical *look, while looking* back at Katie.

Katie reassured Sissy, saying, "It will be all right. I'll see you after lunch on the playground. Go learn something!"

Another time was when Mr. Tatterson came early to pick up Sissy from a sleepover they were having at Katie's house. He needed to tell her that her older brother Corey had been killed in a Bosnian conflict. Her dad hugged her as she *looked over* at Katie, with that same *identical look.*

Today that *same look* back gave Katie hope!

"Ms. Mary Elizabeth Tatterson, you may think you're fooling everyone, but you're not fooling me at all! You're acting out and maybe feeling a little misplaced, but in time you'll find your way back. *And I'll be waiting for you right here!*"

Sissy was still her best friend, even though at this moment, *she was not a good one*! Katie knew that somehow, with God's help, he'll get through to her, letting her know that she was still there for her, just like she was in the third grade and on the day her brother died.

Graduation was a bittersweet occasion for Katie. But with a renewed hope for their friendship, the evening became a little sweeter as her folks took a few more pictures with Katie's new Nikon camera that her Aunt Mart and Uncle Ralph had given her as an early graduation present.

After the photo shoot, they went to Katie's for her mom's prime rib dinner. With the family's help, a feast with all the trimmings was displayed on (two) ten-foot tables. Reverend James gave the blessing. While he was praying, Katie could not help but remember her love for Mrs. James and how she would've loved it if she could've been there. But she could not, since she had died last year, passing away in her sleep.

The crowd said in unison, "Amen!"

After that they filled up their plates to overflowing then scattered all over the house, eating wherever they could find a place to sit or to stand.

It was so packed even Grandma commented, "This house couldn't hold not one more person!"

Oh, if that were only true ... If Sissy would have come, she and Sissy would've gone out on the roof if they had to.

Katie's triple-tiered cake was a present from Aunt Eldee. It was a yellow cake, with coconut custard filling, white fondant, trimmed with pink roses, and written on top was "ISU." The cake was both decadent and delicious too.

It was time for Katie to open her gifts. The first one came from her grandparents. It was a new pair of running shoes. They wanted to give her something practical and one with a joke attached to it!

Because they always said, "They've seldom seen Katie when she wasn't *runnin*!" With their joke being repeated, the guest agreed and joined in with a bunch of laughter.

Next Katie was handed a stack full of greeting cards, most having tens and twenties in them. After the last envelope was opened, her guests got real quiet. She could not help but to notice, some whispering back and forth.

What secret do they have? Katie wondered.

Katie's dad took her by the hand while her mother covered her eyes. They led her through the front door, onto the porch.

When she stopped there, the crowd yelled a deafening "Surprise, surprise!"

And there she was...newly painted a Kelly green color, with new tires, new carpet, and newly upholstered interior. There was even an ISU Bulldog license plate on her front bumper and a "*GOKTGO*" personalized license plate on the rear one. Her dad's vintage Volkswagen Super Beetle today became Katie Vincent's very first car.

Reverend James asked, "Don, she's a *beaut*, but does she run?"

Don replied, "Does she run? She runs better now than when she was new!" Turning to Katie, he asked, "Honey, do you want to take her for a spin?"

He handed her the keys that he secretly had placed on her lucky rabbit-foot keychain.

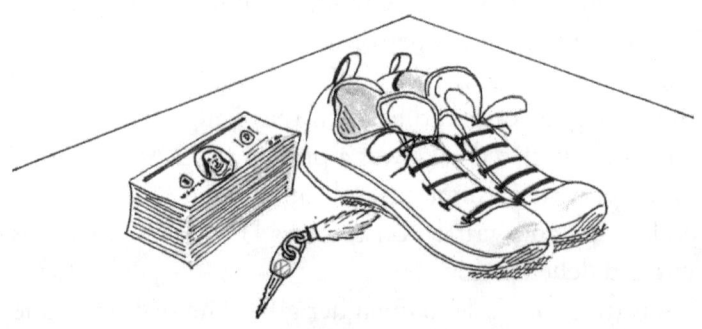

Katie got in and was amazed that everything appeared brand-new and smelled like it too! She put on her seat belt, adjusted the rearview mirror, and started her up.

She hesitated. Then taking off her tiny cross necklace, she hung it on her rearview mirror. Turning to her parents, she said, "Now it's perfect!"

She pulled out of the driveway and headed toward the Dairy Freeze, of course!

Arriving at the Freeze, she sent her dad a text, letting him know where she was and thanked them again with "*xoxoxo*." He turned and showed the text to their party guests, and they all were so happy for the three of them. For most had known that they had been sharing two vehicles for the last couple of years. Many knew what Don Vincent was up to as he worked on his old VW.

For two years, Don has been discouraging Katie from buying a used car, telling her to save her money for her college instead. Today she knew why. "Dad was keeping *a Kelley green secret*!"

With college paid for through scholarships and now a car without a payment, if she would eat a lot of oodles of noodles, resist shopping for clothes, make no extra purchases, and limiting herself to only one extravagance a month, Katie could make it on her savings. Besides, she made a promise to her grandpa that she would not be tempted with one of those burdensome student loans. If she kept her word, he would send her an extra $400 a semester to put toward her books and fees or whatever! After praying and considering the deal, Katie agreed and made a pack with him, promising *no* student loans!

Grandma had already planned on putting Grandpa's check in a care package each semester containing gift cards, coffee, rolls of quarters for Laundromat, laundry detergent, dryer sheets, chocolates, honey, gummy bears, and her favorite chewable vitamins.

Speaking of laundry…Sissy, with a lot of help from Katie, did clean up her act—all except that awful habit she picked up from her Lumberport posse friends: *smoking*. Katie did make her promise to start on the nicotine replacement patch, the one Katie showed her from the pamphlet she had picked up from Doc Conner's office. Katie made Sissy aware of how dangerous the effects of cigarettes were to her health by showing her a photo of a healthy lung versus a smoker's lung. That settled it for Sissy; she was convinced. It took her seeing a photo of a cancerous lung to do it!

Sissy also enrolled in evening classes at Central Bristol Community College (CBCC). She had plans on making good grades so that she could transfer to ISU next year.

Mrs. Rice promised Katie to keep a watchful eye on Sissy. She had watched Sissy's high school life become a train wreck from her repeated losses, one right after another.

Her first loss was as a young girl, losing her older brother. Then she experienced the loss of her grandfather and dad's business due to the failing economy. Next was watching her grandfather's struggle with the sale of his lake property, the lake home that their family made so many memories in. But most of all, Sissy seemed to have lost herself.

Mrs. Rice knew all too well and understood that feeling. She felt it too when she lost her Gerald, fifteen months ago. The only way she did not completely lose it was to resist despair with the help of her best friend, Lorene Carson. For that reason, Mrs. Rice and Lorene both admired the friendship that Katie and Sissy had shared.

Even though Sissy did everything she could possibly do to sabotage it, it was Katie's unconditional love that refused to let her go.

Katie approached Mrs. Rice to ask if she would give Sissy her job once she left for college. She knew Sissy now needed the money, and more than the money, she needed very little idle time on her hands. Days full of school and work—that was just what Sissy needed! If not, she just might relapse into her previous course of self-destruction.

Mrs. Rice agreed to hire her, with two stipulations: first, that none of those rowdy friends of hers from Lumberport would hang around the Freeze, and the second, that she would show up for work on time and give her an honest day's work.

Sissy agreed to the terms of her pending employment. Mrs. Rice told her that she could come by the Freeze Tuesday morning to fill out her employment paperwork, also that she could begin to work part-time until the end of August then she would become a full-time employee when Katie left for college.

Katie said, "Not so fast! Wait a minute, girly girl! You must promise me three things, not just two. First, you must deposit half of your check into your savings account. Remember, the one that our parents opened at the Farmers Federal Bank three years ago? Next, you'll never skip classes and never miss a day of work at the Freeze. And number three, never again will I ever hear that you've been seen hanging out with that riffraff that you used to hang with!"

Sissy hugged her best friend after sealing her promises with a pinky swear.

Sissy Tatterson might have chosen the long road around, concerning their well-thought-out plans for college; however, it was looking promising that they were going to work out after all.

Katie and Sissy sat on Katie's front porch swing, sharing one last cherry twin-pop Popsicle, watching the sun's yellows and reds sit down into Clarion's gray-colored skyline. Then together they packed up Katie's bug for her move to ISU in the morning.

"Oh, one more thing," Sissy said. She handed Katie a box wrapped in hello Kitty wrapping paper.

Katie giggled, saying, "I wonder who wrapped this?"

"It's from me, Austin, and the entire Tatterson clan."

Katie quickly opened it, and much to her surprise, in it was a brand-new Apple laptop computer.

"Are you kidding me? Sissy ... you guys shouldn't have done that."

Sissy said, "I know, it's much too expensive, right?" (while joking and laughing about them being so poor and all!).

Sissy ran to her car's back seat and pulled out a smiley-face gift bag.

"This one's from me!"

Katie reached into a puff of black tissue paper and pulled out that cropped-off Lumberport football jersey in which Sissy paraded down the aisle at their high school graduation. Sissy ran as Katie chased her down laughing. Sissy jumped into her car, and Katie threw the shirt at her! Then Katie ran over to the passenger side and hopped in. There they sat laughing and reminiscing for an hour longer.

They enjoyed going over and highlighting some of their childhood adventures as well as their adolescent dreams, then moving on to their current plan as if it were an executive board meeting. Of course, Katie was the president, and Sissy was the VP. It was after midnight, when the girls decided they both needed to call it a night. So sad that they had to say their last goodbye till summer.

Katie got out of the car. Sissy pulled out, her red brake lights glowing. She turned left at the end of Katie's driveway. Sissy beeped her horn as they traditionally did.

Beep, beep, beep, beep, beep, beep, beep!

Katie's parents were waiting up, drinking a cup of chamomile tea around the kitchen table. Katie showed them her new laptop, telling her mom that she was giving her her old desktop.

Katie said, "Sissy's going to teach you how to use it so you can e-mail me at school!"

Both her mom and dad appeared happy for her and commented, "The computer was a very expensive gift!"

Dad asked, "What's in that bag?" pointing to the smiley-face bag that Katie held in her right hand.

"Oh, it's nothing, it was Sissy just being Sissy!"

And with that answer, Katie ran upstairs.
She quickly put her on pj's and texted her best friend:

> Thanks again for the Apple. Be sure and tell Austin and the whole family that I said, thanks a bunch! Oh, how rude of me. I almost forgot to thank you for the shirt too…Ha-ha-ha! I'm leaving my old computer with Mom. I…kinda committed you into teaching her how to use it, and I'm counting on you to set her up an e-mail account. Show her how to e-mail me at school. That's all!!! Good night!"
>
> KT

Chapter Five

Leaving, *aka* Got to Go Now!

LEAVING—A WORD THAT ALMOST EVERYONE had used in anger at one time or another.

Leaving—a word Katie and Sissy had looked forward to experiencing since they attended Clarion Junior High together.

However, today hearing her mom yell for her dad to come inside because "Katie's *leaving* now" sent a panic throughout Katie's body! That seven-letter word overwhelmed her with a chilling sense of unsurety. *Leaving* left Katie feeling less safe and a little unsure about being all alone in that great *big* world out there.

"Okay, Katie," she encouraged herself, "just calm down! Put one foot in front of the other, and head downstairs! Girl, you made the grades! You've been awarded the scholarships! You worked and saved enough money to cover your living expenses! Anyway…you've already made all the rounds telling your family and friends your *goodbyes!*"

Just mustering up enough courage, Katie made it down the stairway.

Am I really ready? she thought.

With that thought, she knew the roller coaster that was taking her on an emotional ride needed to stop!

Really Katie, just leave!

At that moment, her mom reached in and gave her a big hug of encouragement.

It's like she was reading my mind.

Next she handed Katie a travel mug full of black coffee, a couple frozen bottles of spring water, and a bag lunch full of her favorites: homemade cherry chocolate chip cookies, a granny smith apple, a bag full of gummy bears, two peanut butter and jelly sandwiches on Wonder bread with the crust cut off!

Mom remembered! Remarkable, since I haven't had one of those sandwiches in years.

Also packed in the bag was her unfinished bottle of chewable vitamins.

Tucked inside was a note from her dad saying, "I put a couple of cassettes in the bug if you want to listen to some really good music! They're nothing like your mom's oldies! Love, Daddy."

And there he stood. Dad was at the front door, the door Katie and her mom newly painted a burnt orange. (This was their last ever house project together.) He reminded Katie to check the bug's oil every time she gassed up. His huge calloused hands unfolded… revealing two hundred dollars in twenties. At that moment, Katie's throat froze into a lump. For she knew that money was made by his hard work as a diesel mechanic. His gift to her meant so much more than anything she could ever purchase with that money!

Katie had always known that she was loved. It was that love that has blanketed her, her entire life.

Why, just yesterday her grandmother, full of godly wisdom, encouraged her by saying, "Love is love, chickadee! We'll now just have to experience it from a distance. It's the same love, and the distance, why, they're only roads."

This thought brought Katie a lot of comfort. Yet she thought, *Why not stay here? Why not continue working at the Freeze during the day and take night classes at CBCC with Sissy? Just settle!*

Just thinking those two words made Katie angry.

Just settle? You've got to be kidding me! Ms. Katie Vincent, you've got to shake yourself out of this melancholy state you're in! Get back into reality! You have a paid education to ISU! Your dream of becoming a nurse is literally only four years away! And besides, you won't be alone for long. Sissy plans on visiting this summer, and she'll transfer to ISU next fall! Also, the family will keep in touch! Mom will e-mail! The grandparents will call! Katie, just get in your bug, start the engine, and go! Go walk through your window of opportunity! GOKTGO!

Rev. and Mrs. James had always known and told Katie that she was not the adventurous type but that she had a lot more going for her than she realized. She was a lot smarter than most her age, and if she would only listen to her voice of reason, she'd fulfill God's plan and purpose for her life.

At that instant, she remembered all those encouraging words of wisdom. So she did just as they had suggested. She listened to her voice of reason. She resolved that the best of what God had for her now was in preparing to become a nurse. And with God's help, the rest of her life's story would unfold.

So with her right foot on the gas pedal and her left foot off the clutch, left hand on the steering wheel and right hand on the gearshift knob, Katie left by saying, "Got to go now!"

She passed by the Dairy Freeze on her way out of town. Mrs. Rice, Sissy, and her coworkers had hung a "Good luck, KT!" banner on the Freeze's front sign. They also attached a huge bunch of lime green helium-filled balloons. That front sign was where Mrs. Rice always announced her daily specials. Knowing this, Katie teared up with joy because today it was their way of saying "KT, you are today's daily special!"

With one last look in the bug's rearview mirror, Katie noticed her mom's tiny gold cross hanging there. And driving her VW bug that was full of her daddy's tender loving care, with their symbols of love all around her, she now was ready and able to say *goodbye to her beloved Clarion!*

Katie turned on her favorite FM radio station, Q-90.

Dave announced, "The current temperature is fifty-eight degrees, which will be the high for the day. The low tonight will be forty-two, with north winds at ten miles per hour, and the five-day forecast will be much the same."

Joey, her favorite DJ, came on and announced the next song. It was his pick of the day. Katie hummed along to "This Kiss" by Faith Hill.

Chapter Six

Y2K...and Beyond!

THE WEATHER WAS PLEASANT ENOUGH, but the drive was unpleasantly long. However, Katie did have her adrenaline to keep her company. She was extremely disappointed when her favorite radio station, Q-90, dropped out after only an hour on the road. She really had high hopes that she wouldn't have to say goodbye to them too—*especially Joey*.

Well, there was always her dad's cassettes in the glove compartment—the best of the 1970s and '80s rock and roll and country's greatest hits, featuring Willie Nelson.

"I don't think so!" Katie resisted them.

Instead she opted on playing the game of "search for the next best station" her entire trip to Indiana.

Katie finally made it to Indiana State University. It only took her thirteen hours of driving time, 735 miles, and eight years of planning. Driving straight through, she stopped only for gas and a time or two to stretch her long legs. Thanks mainly to her mom's bagged lunch and a supersized mug of black Maxwell House coffee. She ate all that her mom had packed except for a half of a pb&j sammich (*as she used to call them*).

ISU campus was massive. Katie was so overwhelmed. All the buildings looked the same—red bricks, with mortar, and very tall. Feeling small, Katie had to calm herself down because panic was starting to creep in.

She was thinking to herself, *Surely after orientation and a tour, I'll be able to distinguish their differences according to their purpose. But for now, first things first. I must find a place to park. Then I'll find my way through this maze of tall buildings and find my dorm.*

Thanks to another student, a junior classman, he gave her good directions to her dorm (dorm building number 12).

Once inside, the dorm counselor welcomed Katie by presenting her with an admission packet and her room key.

"Your parking sticker is in your packet. If I were you, Ms. Vincent, I'd get it on your car first thing. You don't want to end your very first day with a parking violation, now, do you?"

"No, ma'am, I sure don't!"

"Okay then, your room is down that hall. Turn right, and it's the second door on the left...number 11A."

Katie would be sharing a room with another freshman. All she knew about her was that her name Marsha Talabruso. Katie located her room then fumbled with the door key, finally getting it to open.

There stood a beautiful blond, looking like a model from *GLAM Magazine*.

"Katie?"

"Marsha?"

Abruptly, Marsha began to talk *"at"* Katie.

"I've been waiting for you! I just stayed here as a favor I owed to our beloved dorm counselor. That's your side of the room, and this...is mine. Don't touch my stuff! And I'll not be touching yours! In fact, we'll seldom be seeing one another. I'll be attending classes and out with my friends the rest of the time. I stay overnight with my boyfriend at the Colonial Apartment Complex in the city. Almost all my stuff is there. I only keep a few photos and clothes here to give an appearance that I live here should my parents ever find time in their busy schedule to pay me a visit. It's the firm's dime that's paying for this place. Do you know what I mean? So this is our little secret. Got it?"

Katie answered, "I understand."

"Fine then, this place is all yours. I'm late for my appointment at the nail salon across town."

Marsha dashed out, leaving a trail of expensive perfume behind her. Katie looked down at her hands and nails. They looked a little rough around their edges.

"Oh well," she said. Turning her attention to her new home, Katie took her parking permit sticker out of her admissions packet and walked back to her car and applied it to her bug's windshield in the upper-left corner as she had been directed.

She made three trips back and forth, back and forth, back and forth, moving in her stuff.

"Marsha, Marsha, Marsha!"

Katie was not at all impressed with Ms. Marsha Whirlwind! There was absolutely no possibility of them ever becoming friends. Katie was glad that she was not going to be around.

"Why, she didn't even offer to give me a helping hand with my stuff!"

Giving no more attention to Marsha, Katie noticed the time on her watch.

"Oh no, Mom is probably worried sick because I haven't called her yet! I promised her that I would as soon as I got here. And boy, is my stomach growling, it sounds like a hungry grizzly's in there."

Munching on a bag of chips and sipping on a Coke she got out of a nearby vending machine, she called home.

"Mom, I made it, I'm here!"

"How was the drive? ... Did you have any trouble finding it?... Dad wants to know, how did the bug run? ... Is your room nice? ... Have you meet your roommate yet?...Is she nice?...What time is your first class Monday morning?...Do you need anything?...Did you forget anything?"

After answering her string of questions, as usual, Katie's mom told her that she knew how important it was for her *Little Miss Independent* to do this all on her own, reminding Katie that if she ever needed them, they would come.

"Yes, Mom! I know, and I love you both for that."

Hanging up the phone, Katie felt both physically and mentally drained. She plopped down sideways on her small dorm bed and *zzzz*...

Katie woke up in a puddle of drool the next day.

"It can't be noon!"

She sprung to her feet, suddenly feeling like she had a bad case of jet lag. She knew about jet lag from experience because she had a bad case of it after flying to the southern part of Mexico. She traveled there with her WCBC youth group to hold a mission's sidewalk outreach in several underprivileged villages there. She also knew the antidote for it, was food and plenty of rest.

It's Sunday. If she were back home in Clarion, she would be attending WCBC, surrounded by both family and friends. Instead, she was reading through her admission packet, finding two complimentary coupons. Each coupon was for a personal pizza and two cans of Coke. Katie was in luck...Momma Roz's Pizzeria was close by, and she delivered!

"So that takes care of lunch and supper too."

She ate lunch and napped. She ate supper and napped again, thanking God at each mealtime for Momma's peperoni pizza slices and Coke's cola.

"Amen!"

The following week whizzed by. Katie had been schooled more than just scholastically. She learned real quick that college was not high school. Hardly any supervision. Not having to answer to anyone. Her definition of college was, "You either get it or not, it's all your own doing." High school was just as much a social club as it was a learning facility. Here at ISU, everybody was buzzing around preoccupied with urgent looks on their faces. As far as she could tell, there was not much socializing going on here.

Fortunately, Katie did meet a nice girl from West Virginia. She lived in the same dorm on the second floor, in room number 9B. Her name was Kimberly Chrislip. She was a senior and a nursing major too. Kimberly invited Katie to the ISU campus church next Sunday morning.

Katie accepted the invitation, saying, "I'll meet you there, just save me a seat."

Katie woke up early Sunday morning, styled her hair, and applied pink translucent lip gloss to her lips. She wore the lavender dress with matching shoes that she wore to her high school graduation.

Feeling real good about the day, Katie happily entered the worship service with a bounce in her step. Much to her surprise, the music was very loud, and almost every student in attendance was dressed much too casual to be going to church. She was uncomfortable and feeling out of place, but it was too late to leave because Kimberly had spotted her and came rushing over.

"Come on, I saved you a seat. I want you to meet a few of my Christian friends."

Really! Katie thought.

"I might have known it. We're sitting up front in the second row."

By now Katie felt that *all* eyes were upon her…"*the new girl.*" *Yes*, the new girl on campus that was overly dressed to impress!

She was on display, thinking, *Okay, people, take a good look!*

At that moment, she felt like the character Rebecca Warner in the 1993 Pauley Shore movie *Son in Law*.

She made it through service, and afterward, Katie said to herself, "I really, really, really do miss Reverend James *a lot*!"

She went back to her dorm, with no tasty Sunday supper to enjoy. Instead, she'd have warmed-up leftover pizza and drink a cold glass of milk.

Having no one to talk to, Katie looked in the mirror as she pulled her hair back into a comfortable ponytail, saying, "Katie, what are you waiting for? Isn't it time to do something?"

To avoid the state of boredom she was slipping into, Katie grabbed that cold slice of pizza, placed it on a napkin, and headed out, walking toward the university's administration building. In its foyer was the campus's only jobs bulletin board.

There she reached for a yellow Post-it note, posted there by the Gingerbread Café. It read, "Wanted: Cashier/Server. Minimum Wage. Apply in Person. Corner of Center and Highland Avenues."

She took the note with her and walked back to her dorm to pray.

After her last freshman orientation class the next morning, Katie had an hour-long break. That was when she decided to walk toward the café. It was conveniently located only one hundred steps from her dorm. She carried with her a newly printed résumé. She wore a pair of jeans and her red, white, and blue patriotic Dairy Freeze T-shirt.

She got the job! The café's owner, Tonie Cameron, appeared laid-back and very cool. She had light reddish-brown cornrows and was dressed in vintage hippie clothing. Looking at her, Katie thought that era must have been her glory days. Both she and her employees appeared nice enough. Their only work uniform was a red plaid apron with a gingerbread cookie name badge. Katie was told that Tonie and her manager, Jo Ann, were both ISU grads. They both loved the area so much that they decided to stay. The café was their dream, and it had been open for six years. Not too shabby, considering most restaurants didn't make it past their one-year anniversary date.

Tonie was well known as a smart small-business owner that provided much needed part-time work for the ISU student body. Katie loved hearing her success story and considered it a privilege to be given the opportunity to work there—not to mention the fact that both Tonie and Jo Ann were willing to work around her busy class schedule.

Perfect! It was just perfect. Katie would once again be around people, her kind ... the chitchatty kind, not just professor after professor talking and overloading her with a lot of facts she had to commit to memory. And the food...she'd be able to eat salads, hot soups, rolls, and muffins too! (as these are all a part of her benefits package) Plus the money she'd be saving was to put toward her and Sissy's apartment that they planned on sharing next year.

Excited...Katie ran back to her dorm. She had just enough time to call her mom and tell her the good news.

Her parents' phone rang. And guess who answered? Sissy did! Both girls couldn't believe it!

"What're the odds of this happening?" Katie said. "Sissy, what are you doing there?"

"Why am I here, you ask? I'm here because of you...remember? I just finished showing your mom how to use your old computer. Austin is here too! He's setting the thing up downstairs and has her e-mail account up and running as well—well, hopefully. Austin says hi, he hopes you're liking school. He's good when it comes to this computer thing. He's taking classes at CBCC in computer programming. Man, the kid is smart. Why, he's borderline genius. How're things up north?"

"Well, things here are going much better now that I have a job. Please don't you tell Mom, I want to."

Sissy said, "Okay."

"I'm going to be saving for our new apartment. I can hardly wait. How about you?"

Sissy replied, "Me too…Katie, I have to give the phone to your mom now. She's standing here and is about to pass out if she doesn't get to talk to you. Love you, kid!"

Katie replied, "Love you too!"

"Hi, Mom."

"Katie, is everything all right?"

"I just got a job."

"Where?"

"It's close by at a cute little corner café."

"Katie, can you manage both your classes and work too? I can't believe I even asked you that question, I know you can!"

"The owner is so nice. She's even going to work around my class schedule. This is an answer to my prayers."

"I'm glad for you honey. If you have a minute, Austin says he needs to tell you something."

"Katie, I just wanted to tell you that I know now where you got all of your smarts from, you got them from your mom! She's really a quick study! I'll prove it to you. Just check your e-mail later, she's sending you a message. It's her first one, and she wanted it to go to you. Be careful up there. Let's keep in touch, okay?…Here's your mom."

Austin handed the phone back to Mrs. Vincent.

"Mom, I gotta run, can't be late."

"Just one more thing," she told Katie. "Dad says to tell you that he loves you and that he misses you a lot."

Just hearing what her dad had said caused Katie to tear up.

"Love you guys too!"

"Katie, remember to check your e-mail!"

"I will, I'll check it after my last class. I gotta go now!"

(You got mail!)

From: Vincent3@aol.com
To: Katie356@aol.com

Hello, honey. This is a test. I know, just what you need is another test. Ha Ha Ha! Message me back so I'll know that this went through. Grandma says, she needs your mailing address. She wants to send you your first care package.

Love,
Mom & Dad too!

P.S. You was right! (Again) I should've learned to use the computer years ago.

(Reply.)

From: Katie356@aol.com
To: Vincent3@aol.com

Mom, I got it! I am so proud of you. What's important now is that you have learned how to use a computer! You're no longer a dinosaur…sorry for calling you one. What does dad think of all of this? Tomorrow will be my first day at the café. It looks like it's going to be busier there than a day at the Freeze. This may sound just a little messed up, but here goes, "The café felt a little like home to me."
My snail mail address is: 1000 Center Ave., Dorm #12, Room 11A, Morgantown, Indiana, 24017.

Love ya,
Katie

P.S. Tell Dad I miss him too and that the bug's running great!

To: ALTatterson@aol.com
From: Katie356@aol.com

    Austin, thanks again for helping my mom with her computer set up. I should have known that Sissy would drag you in on her obligation. I hope school is working out for you too! I might need to ask you for some help with my new Apple, as I'm still learning its applications. Is that OK?

Katie

P.S. Did Sissy ever let know you that I said thanks for the graduation gift? If not, I am telling you now, "Thanks for my computer. It's exactly what I need to keep up, but I guess you already knew that, didn't you?" I know this was your gift idea, wasn't it? It wasn't Sissy's…Hers was a cropped off t-shirt! Ha Ha Ha!! Ask her about that one.

(Reply.)

From: ALTatterson@aol.com
To: Katie356@aol.com

    No, she didn't. I just figured that you told her thanks anyway. You can contact me anytime! Sissy told me about her T-shirt prank gift to you. Do you think my Sis will ever grow up? Don't answer that one! Only God has the answer to that one!

Only time will tell.

Austin

From: Sissy4short@aol.com
To: Katie356@aol.com

Hey girl, we took care of that AOL thing with your mom. One more thing, I helped her remove all of those pink and purple glitter hearts and your *"hello! Kitty"* stickers off your monitor. Have you heard Brittney Spears new song yet? Speaking of music, guess who Austin and I had to listen to all day yesterday? Your mom's Leslie Gore record. She also asked us both to go with her next Saturday to go buy a mobile phone just like yours. She does not want an outdated one like your dad's work phone.

Love you xoxo Katie girl.

Ta Ta for now!

Sissy

P.S. Don't freak! I got a few blue streaks dyed in my hair. Mrs. Rice just shakes her head. I think I look way too cool for Clarion, Alabama. Austin took a picture of me and it's on its way to you now. Look for it in your granny's box.

(Reply.)

From: Katie356@aol.com
To: Sissy4short@aol.com

    Not my stickers! I won those in youth group for answering correctly all those difficult Bible quiz questions, remember?
    And to answer your question, here, the girls I know (which is a total of six) listen to the Dixie Chicks and Third Day, not Disney's Brittney Spears. I am so glad to hear that my mom is evolving. How's your family doing? How's the Freeze?

                                      HUGS
                                        KATIE

P.S. Blue streaks, really? You're just kidding, right?

To: Katie356@aol.com
From: ALTatterson@aol.com

    I forgot to tell you something. Remember Bucky Stevens? He's Kimmy Steven's older brother. He went to ISU his freshman and sophomore years before transferring to Cal State. Their cousin Belinda is a freshman at ISU this year. Small world, isn't it? If you want, look her up. She's a mechanical engineer major. Dad's yelling for me. I need to go and help him make a delivery. Must go for now!

                                        Austin

"Now it's back to the real world!" Katie proclaimed, gesturing with both hands in the air.

Her daily checklist went as follows:

- ✓ Attend classes
- ✓ Work at the Gingerbread Café
- ✓ Computer work in the evening
- ✓ Prep for next day classes
- ✓ Nights—get some sleep
- ✓ Sundays—attend Rock-n-Roll Church

"All of this in just twenty-four hours. Time here in Indiana speeds by a whole lot faster than it did in Alabama."

Katie had gotten used to this time change of her own choosing because Mr. and Mrs. Don Vincent's only child was a goal-orientated young lady. The latest goal that she had set for herself was to stay in Indiana and work through all the next major holidays and the summer months too. Tonie recently rewarded her excellent job performance and superior work ethics by naming Katie Jo Ann's assistant. She even received a modest bonus presented to her in a "Job Well Done!" Hallmark greeting card.

She kept in close contact, as promised, with her parents, grandparents, Sissy, and occasionally with Austin (mainly via e-mails).

(You got mail!)

>From: Vincent3@aol.com
>To: Katie356@aol.com

Dear Katie,

How's things going with you? This year's school clock is winding down, isn't it? Are you getting enough to eat? Remember to brush your teeth. I can't believe I just wrote that one. Oh my, I still must remind myself that you're not a little girl anymore. But rather, you're a successful college student. This week I gave up my part-time job. Mine and your dad's pace of life has really slowed down. We both are praying, asking what's next for us. Now, we don't want you to think that this has anything to do with you going off to school and choosing to stay away this summer. Well, it does have a tiny part to do with it. Regardless, we both knew that this time would come. But for us, it came much too soon. We were just too busy living everyday life to plan. The blessing is, with no plan, we are now free to choose what we believe is best for us. We're free to fill our free time as the Lord directs. I saw Sissy at the Freeze this afternoon. She says she has some news to tell you and that she plans on calling you around 8 tonight. So listen for her call.

Keep us in your prayers,
Love, Mom

Sissy kept her word and called Katie at 8:32 p.m. (That's a switch!) Katie thought she was mainly calling just to hear her voice, since they hadn't talked in a couple of weeks. Why no phone calls? They both were trying to keep their phone bill down.

Sissy apologized for not calling sooner, informing Katie that Mrs. Rice had been needing her to work longer hours.

"Girl, it's really hard filling your shoes around here, both here at the Freeze and at WCBC too!"

Sissy's main motive for calling became clear. It was to chat about their new reverend, Reverend Wade Foxx. She also made sure Katie knew that she'd also been putting in a lot of hours volunteering at the church. Since Katie had always preached to her about thinking of others…before herself! And the "others" Sissy was apparently thinking about…was singular and was single; his name was Reverend Foxx.

Next on her agenda was to see how Katie would react to her news about putting off her move to Indiana in the fall. Of course, she also wanted to inform her best friend on how well she was doing at CBCC.

Sissy was proud to say, "I've been showing up for all of my classes, and I'm even passing all of them!" (Just as she had promised Katie she would.) "Katie, I want to thank you again for everything! My life is so much better with you in it! Okay, enough of that mushy stuff. So…we're okay, right?"

"You know we're okay, silly girl!"

Katie was okay with the fact that more than likely, Sissy would *not* be joining her in Indiana. She was pleasantly surprised. Katie all along had had a strong suspicion that it just might work out this way but never let it be known to anyone. For Sissy had a history of being flighty and a little wishy-washy.

However, this time was different.

For the first time, Sissy was refreshingly standing firm in her decision-making, solid with her decision to help Mrs. Rice when she needed her the most (sure, sounds familiar, doesn't it?) and to stay focused in school and dedicated in her volunteering efforts at the church even though Katie was convinced that Sissy had an ulterior motive.

Could it be?

"My best friend just may be growing up." She had obligations in Alabama and cared about fulfilling them!

Happy for Sissy but a little sad for herself, Katie reassured her friend to do what she felt was best and how very proud she was of her! By letting Sissy out of their arrangement, Sissy *now* had an opportunity to really excel back home in Alabama! And as for Katie, she was learning to stand on her own (singular).

(You got mail!)

> From: Vincent3@aol.com
> To: Katie356@aol.com
>
> It's been over a week since we chatted. I tried to call, but no answer. You must have worked over. You're right, e-mailing is better for us too.

Dad did it! He retired. No more greasy uniforms to wash. That's the upside. The downside is that he has a lot of time on his hands. Especially since the bug is up and running. Dad says to let you know that his metric tools are available if anything on the VW should need *fixin'*. He's spending a lot of time napping, snoring his way through Sports TV. I am strongly encouraging him to do something, anything but mildew. He just told me this morning during breakfast that he's considering coin collecting again. He collected coins when he was a teenager. In that same chest where my Suzi-Q and your *Emmalea* is, he still has a Tiparillo cigar box full of his old coins. They're under that stack of my old black-and-white photographs. Remember them? Years ago, I put his coins there for safekeeping, just in case. Well, just in case has arrived, only taking thirty-nine years to get here. I read in Sunday's Mobile Times, that in three weeks there's going to be a coin show at the Mobile Armory. We are thinking about going and making a day of it.

XOXO
Mom

(Reply.)

From: Katie356@aol.com
To: Vincent3@aol.com

    Mom, I'm glad for Dad. But what about you?

Katie

(Reply.)

From: Vincent3@aol.com
To: Katie356@aol.com

    Thanks for asking, honey. Just yesterday, I was in Gabe's shopping. (By the way, his granddaughter Ginny was working at the checkout counter, and she asked about you. She said to tell you, "Hi.") When I was there I bought a Rand McNally map of the United States. Today, I've been looking through it. I told Dad I'd like to travel to all fifty states. Surprisingly he said, "While we're in Mobile, we can go by the AAA office and join. Then we can talk with them, possibly to plan our first trip." Imagine that! I'm so excited. We have never been anywhere. Hey, I've been wanting to ask, how's your roommate Marsha? You never mention her.

                                Love, Mom

    Mr. and Mrs. Don Vincent's first trip away from their home sweet home Alabama was traveling to Indiana. (No surprise there!) They pulled into ISU, and it was just as Katie had described it. It looked like a city of its own. They came as a surprise to Katie! It has been two months since their retirement, and wild horses could not keep them away any longer!
    "Katie's at her anatomy class," her dorm counselor informed them.
    So they decided they would wait there in the lobby.
    "She doesn't come home directly from class. She goes on to work at the café, and gets in around nine o'clock."
    Hearing her give such details concerning Katie's schedule made them feel so much better about Katie being at ISU. Knowing those watchful eyes were on their daughter's every move made them relax some.

Katie's dad was not at all surprised that Katie would run directly from class to work. "That's my Katie!" he said, "Always running!"

At his request, the counselor gave the Vincents directions to the Gingerbread Café. They arrived, introducing themselves to both Tonie and Jo Ann. Tonie told them that they had forty-five minutes before Katie's shift began.

Tonie treated them to a ham-and-cheese sandwich on rye bread and a bowl of four-bean soup. Meanwhile, Jo Ann ran out to the Party Store two blocks away to purchase a bunch of helium-filled balloons and some noise makers. When she returned, they only had minutes until Katie arrived.

Katie punched in as the café's close-knit group yelled, "Surprise!"

Katie spotted her mom and dad standing by the cookie display case and was elated! Everyone in the place was full of cheers. Her parents were shocked to see Katie's short hair, just as they too were surprised to see her ten-pound weight gain. She told them that she was going to tell them and that she had just gotten her haircut yesterday.

Then Tonie laughed and said, "It's her freshman ten! She sure looks cute in short hair, doesn't she?"

Her dad quickly replied, "I am just glad there's no blue streaks in it!"

Katie missed her parents but did not know how much until now. Tonie clocked Katie out, covering her shift, sending the three Vincent's on their merry way. Returning to her dorm room, her momma asked again about Marsha. Katie told her that over Memorial Day weekend, her parents showed up and she was nowhere to be found on campus. Their dear dorm counselor squealed on her. That's when her father gave her an ultimatum.

She could stay here at ISU with no money, with all funds being cut off, or she could travel back with them to New York and attend the New York Fashion Design Institute in downtown Manhattan. She chose New York and followed the money home!

Katie changed her clothes and gave her parents an ISU grand tour, introducing them to her new way of life. She enjoyed showing them around campus as well as downtown Morgantown. Katie spent most of the next two days with her parents in their hotel room at the newly built Microtel Hotel located in the heart of town. They rode in a taxi and even the trolley. They enjoyed a beautiful sunset from the rooftop of the Gieco Insurance skyscraper. Her parents were introduced to sushi and fish tacos. (Her dad was not impressed at all.)

Katie was told that her childhood home was going to be put up for sale. This was news her parents had preferred not to break to her over the phone or in an e-mail. She was sad but understood that it was too much house for just the two of them.

"We have accumulated a lot of stuff that we really don't need anymore," her mom told her.

Katie was asked to think if there was anything that she would want to keep and that they'd send it to her when Sissy moved up in the fall.

"How's that going?" they asked. "Do you two have a final plan?"

"As a matter of fact, yes, I do." Showing them an apartment key, Katie explained, "I'm supposed to move in tomorrow. I've rented a fully furnished apartment, and you're here just in time to help me move!"

"Well…lucky us!"

Mr. and Mrs. Vincent helped their only child move her things into her cozy little furnished loft apartment only ten minutes off campus.

She told them, "I didn't even have to sign a lease. It's just month to month, so if it doesn't work out, I can just as easily move on."

She informed them also that Sissy told her that more than likely, she would not be moving to Indiana. They both said that they didn't get to see Sissy much anymore, especially since Mrs. Rice had been diagnosed with Alzheimer's and that Sissy had been working a lot lately.

"Katie, you would be so proud of her! She's taking on her responsibilities at the Freeze and has turned out to be a dependable worker, just as you thought she would. Katie, to have a friend like you, Sissy Tatterson is one lucky young lady. Oh yes, there's something else you need to know. The blue in her hair is gone, and she's finally quit smoking too!"

"How's her family?" asked Katie.

"Well, they sold their home in Clarion, settling all their debts, and we hear that they're moving to Denver, Colorado. Remember the skiing trips their family used to take to Vail? There they met a businessman, and they had kept in touch throughout the years. Ernie will be working for him at his lumber processing plant in Littleton, just outside of Denver."

Katie said, "It's good to hear that they're back on their feet and are doing well again!"

"They ask about you all the time. Here's their cell phone number, you should give them a call."

"And Austin?" Katie asked.

"He graduated early. You already knew that he was taking evening classes at CBCC with Sissy, didn't you? Recently, he too has moved and attends the University of Alabama majoring in computer science. As for Sissy, she lives in Aunt Mart's boarding house. But you probably already knew that, didn't you?"

With Katie's move complete, her parents were ready to leave. Tearfully the three Vincent's said their goodbyes as her parents left, traveling toward their next adventure…the Great Smoky Mountains in Tennessee.

(You got mail!)

>From: Katie356@aol.com
>To: ALTatterson@aol.com

>Austin, my mom and dad surprised me with a visit. They told me you're attending the University of Alabama. I didn't know you were such a geek? Computer science, uh? I'm impressed. Remember how Sissy and I used to tease you all the time? Sissy would say that you got all the Tatterson's intelligence genes but that she got all the Tatterson's good looks that looked good in jeans!
>Katie (Roll Tide!)

(Reply.)

From: ALTatterson@aol.com
To: Katie356@aol.com

Sissy did tell me she was staying in Clarion. Are you OK with that? As for me, I guess someone had to be the smart one! Ha! Ha! I really got interested in computers after all that Y2K talk was going around. I'm late for class. Bye for now.

Austin

(You got mail!)

From: Katie356@aol.com
To: Vincent3@aol.com

Mom, I took a couple of weeks to think about your question. I only want to keep two things. That old chest with *Emmalea* in it and your old record player and records (especially, the Nancy Sinatra and Neil Sedaka ones). That is, if you don't mind parting with them? Oh yes, you'll be glad to hear that I called the Tatterson's. They sounded great! It appears that all their losses are behind them now. Thanks for giving me their number. They asked if we could visit them soon in Colorado. They say that they have more than enough room for all of us to stay with them. They did say that even though they had been through a lot, they were always aware that God was keeping them and that Jesus loved them. Tonight, I'm making your recipe for spaghetti and meatballs. It's my first official meal here in my new home. Tonie, her boyfriend, Neil, and Jo Ann will be joining me. Thanks for teaching me how to cook!

>Love, Your Katie

P.S. Yesterday, a child was choking on a piece of chicken at the Café. I could save him by using the *Heimlich Maneuver*. This is what I want to do with the rest of my life. Now, I am 100% sure that I made the right decision to major in nursing. It felt so natural for me. Everyone else at the Café was in a panic! Much to my surprise, I remained calm and took control of the situation. In the back of my mind, I've always wondered if I could do it and I did. (By the way, it's a lot different than fixing a doll baby's leg, that's for sure!! How Nurse Margie must have gotten a big tickle out of my story that day in Doc Connor's office!)

(Reply.)

From: Vincent3@aol.com
To: Katie356@aol.com

We always knew that whatever you put your mind to, you would be good at it. It's always been our pleasure, being your mom and dad. To answer your question, Nurse Margie and I both got such a tickle from you on that day. Remember you thought for sure you were ready to start "fixing people" right then! Nurse Margie encouraged you by talking you into going to school first! I thought those was the items you'd be wanting to keep so…I already put *Emmalea's* chest, record player, and all my records in storage for you. The realtor plans on showing the house in two weeks, after your dad does a little painting and has new no-wax linoleum floors put down in the kitchen and in both bathrooms. We're planning on going to the Gulf of Mexico while the house is being sold. Our agent helped us rent a beachfront condo at Gulf Shores, Alabama. There's someone at the door. It may be the floor shop! Got to go!

Mom

It was official. Katie was now a sophomore. News from home was that Mrs. Rice had passed away and that she left the Freeze to Sissy in her will. It was in God's plan! He knew it was best for Sissy to stay in Clarion after all; it suited her! She was settled, and so was Katie in her life at ISU. Both the Freeze and Morgantown, Indiana, had something in common. They both had elevated those two close friends into full grown-up status.

All of Clarion was buzzing about Sissy's inheritance. They all agreed, and even Mrs. Betts too, that Mrs. Rice made a wise decision in leaving Sissy the Dairy Freeze. Katie was very happy with Sissy's new blessing!

Katie now knew the answer to the question why Sissy didn't move to Indiana. God had resolved the situation, and the biblical scripture that read, "Lord, not my will be done, but yours," was the truth.

We must always remember to pray and ask him because Father *does* know *best* and his will will be done! He's God…He already knows our futures.

And for those who allow him, he's a good character builder also. (*You need proof… just look at the characters in this story.*)

Other news from Clarion was that Sissy has gotten hyperactive in church again. She was assisting Reverend Foxx with his transition into the WCBC routine, since Reverend James retired. In Sissy's last e-mail, she mentioned that her new pastor's name was Reverend Wade Foxx.

Today she wrote and told Katie, "He sure is a *fox*!"

"That girl, all grown up, right? My Popsicle-eating best friend who once had blue hair with a deception going on…regarding how the dent in her mom's car really got there. *Lives on!*"

Katie's last class of the day was canceled due to her pharmacology professor having to be hospitalized because of dehydration and the flu. So she opted to go into work early and bake a double batch of the café's gingerbread cookies.

When in walked a good-looking tall young man in his late twenties. He approached Katie with a poster board in his right hand. Katie brushed off the powdered sugar from both of her arms and from the front of her plaid apron. She recognized him. He'd eaten lunch there a few times but was always accompanied by two older gentlemen in business suits.

He introduced himself as Kurk Lavathian. Katie pointed out that he always ordered chicken parm, on a croissant with a large mocha latte—one sugar.

Impressed, he said, "Now that you know who I am, what's your name?"

She answered, "Katie. Katie Vincent. And to answer your question, Tonie does allow customers to hang posters on that back wall, but they must come down the first of each month."

He said, "That would be just fine."

He ordered a mocha latte, with one sugar, to go. As he was leaving, he stopped and gave Katie a flirty second glance, saying, "Thanks again, Ms. Katie—Katie Vincent."

Curiously, Katie ran over to read his poster. It read,

> Thank you, citizens of Morgantown, for voting for me. It was a pleasure running as your city councilman. (Maybe next time.) Signed Kurk Lavathian – KurktheISU@aol.com

(You got mail!)

> From: Vincent3@aol.com
> To: Katie356@aol.com
>
> Good morning, Katie! Did you get Grandma and Grandpa's package? I was just over at their house. You should give them a call. Grandpa has a chest cold. Grandma was making him his favorite strawberry Jell-O and some of her homemade chicken broth. They said they missed hearing from you.
>
> Mom

(Reply.)

> From: Katie356@aol.com
> To: Vincent 3@aol.com
>
> I did get their package. She sent it through UPS this time. I just called them. Grandma is taking good care of Grandpa. He's in really good hands. I also thanked her for the green mittens and scarf she made for me. When I opened the box, she had stuffed one of the mittens … to make it look like a real hand. Then she placed Grandpa's check in it. She has such good ideas!

Mom, her creativity trickled down to you, didn't it? Wasn't it sweet of her to remember that I love green?

XOXO
Katie

Sitting at her computer desk, she logged off. That was when her elbow knocked off her Bible onto the apartment's hardwood floor. It was the very same Bible that Mrs. James gave her when she and Sissy went forward at WCBC. Three photographs spilled out onto the floor in the process. They were taken at her high school graduation: one with her parents, one with her grandparents, and one with Sissy, Austin, and the entire Vincent family. She kissed each one and put them back where they belonged. Then the doorbell rang.

She looked through her door's peephole. It was Kurk Lavathian! She was reserved in answering but did so (only by cracking the door open with the security chain still intact).

"What are you doing here? And how do you know where I live?"

"Can I come in and I'll answer both?"

She paused ... Then Katie let Kurk in. He proceeded in telling her that he got her address from a waitress at the Gingerbread Café.

Kurk pleaded with her, "Now, don't be too upset with your coworker. After all, I told her a little white lie that you had already given me your address and that I had lost it. And with my charm, she simply couldn't resist giving it to me! No harm done, right?"

Katie made a fresh pot of coffee, and they sat for a couple of hours getting to know one another. Katie talked about nursing, her family, Sissy, Clarion, her church, and the Dairy Freeze. Kurk talked about his ambitions and politics.

Leaving, Kurk asked Katie out on a date that Friday night. He wanted her to go with him to the Blue Ridge Citizen Park, where Morgantown's Chamber of Commerce would be showing an outdoor movie, *All the President's Men*. This would be in celebration of the park's fiftieth anniversary. His frat brother, Tom Nelson, was in the National Guard—Color Guard. He'd been chosen to lead the crowd in reciting of the Pledge of Allegiance, just before the movie would begin.

She answered, "I get off at five, so I can go with you."

"It's a date then, I'll pick you up at six."

Kurk asked Katie to pack a cooler with snacks and drinks.

Katie said, "That would be no problem. One more thing." She asked, "Have you ever ridden in a VW bug? Why don't we take my car?"

"Okay, sounds like fun! Don't you think I need your phone number and your e-mail address?"

She willingly gave him both. The next few days could not have gone by any slower.

Friday morning.

(You got mail!)

>From: KurktheISU@aol.com
>To: Katie356@aol.com

>Are we still on for tonight?

>   Kurk

(Reply)

>From: Katie356@aol.com
>To: KurkISU@aol.com

>Can hardly wait, see you here at six.

>   Katie

(She really should have signed it, *Smitten Katie*!)

Friday at six o'clock sharp, Prince Charming was standing outside Katie's door. He was carrying a small pink gift bag in his hand.

What could that be? Katie thought.

Walking in, Kurk handed his gift to Katie. She pulled out a Rubik's Cube.

"You remembered!"

For it was next on Katie's list of personal goals that she had shared with Kurk just a few nights ago.

"Kurk, you get the cooler, and if it's all right with you, I want to take my Rubik's Cube."

Katie planned on trying to solve it in between movie scenes and snacking. But she failed. She could only get all red squares on one side. She quit for the night by putting it alongside her dad's cassettes in her glove compartment.

All the President's Men who? What movie? It was unable to hold Katie's attention because hers was now on Kurk. He was simply charming. He put the *prince* in *charming*! Kurk…his smell, his hands, his Gucci loafers, and just the fact that he was showing an interest in her at all made Katie blush.

Katie pulled into her apartment's assigned parking space, and Kurk gave her a kiss on the cheek. All she could come up with was to invite him to church on Sunday.

He said, "I can't. Sunday I need to go and visit my parents, but I can come over Monday evening. We can watch *Jeopardy*, and you can order a pizza."

While *Jeopardy* was not her idea of a second date, to have another opportunity to be with Kurk, she'd watch an entire evening *full of game shows*! However, she absolutely refused to eat another pizza—simply because her freshman ten came from the calories Momma Roz put into her delicious pizza slices.

So she asked Kurk, "Why don't I cook us a meal?"

Quickly Kurk let her know…"I don't like pork, tuna, celery, tofu, mayonnaise, and radishes."

She answered, "That's all right. I'll make chicken and dumplings and a salad without celery and radishes. Is raspberry vinaigrette dressing okay with you?"

Up to that point, Katie's life of being on her own had been successful by her using wisdom as her guide: saving money and spending it sparingly, making passing grades by showing up to class prepared, making good choices—that is, until Kurk entered the picture.

Since then her judgments had become somewhat clouded. Let me explain. Katie continued to see Kurk only when it fit into *his* busy schedule. He dominated all conversations by centering them around himself and his plans. Her mom even warned her not to lose her focus. However, she trusted Katie because she had never seen her Katie fail to use sound judgments regarding relationships.

Tonie didn't care much for Kurk. She let Katie know that she didn't know exactly why…but that "it was just a feeling she had in her gut."

Katie laughed it off by saying, "Oh, it's just a little indigestion from eating Jo Ann's cooking!"

Then they all had a good laugh at Jo Ann's expense. But their cheerfulness did not remove Tonie's watchful eye!

Laughter was in abundance as Thanksgiving approached. Katie's mom and dad were loving their stay at the Gulf, so much so that they had decided to stay until mid-March. Why mid-March, you might ask? That was when countless high school and college students invade the beach celebrating spring break. And Mr. and Mrs. Vincent wanted no part of it! They still had no serious buyer for their homeplace. Katie could take a train to the Gulf and spend Thanksgiving there, as her parents had suggested. But she chose to stick with her goal to work at the café instead.

It was ISU's Thanksgiving break, and the foot traffic at the café had slowed down significantly. Most of ISU's student population had traveled home for their turkey dinner. Katie's hours had to be cut back, but that was okay with her. She always had her savings to fall back on.

"Heck," she said, "Anyway, I need the rest more than the money…I'm exhausted!"

It was the Tuesday before Thanksgiving, and Tonie decided to close shop, for an early snowfall was in the forecast. Katie decided to go home to watch for its arrival from her living room window's vantage point.

Simply beautiful was God's masterpiece, as his powdered snow began to fall everywhere.

Katie couldn't believe her eyes. Kurk was pulling up in front of her building in his black Porsche sports car. Kurk called her on her phone, asking her to come down, telling her that he had a surprise for her. Katie bundled up and flew out her front door. Kurk tossed some snow at her. She retaliated…by scooping up handfuls of the white fluff, tossing it onto his brown wool overcoat.

Kurk ran away from her to his sports car. He pulled out a dozen long-stemmed red roses. He pulled Katie in close and kissed her. I mean, he really kissed her. Katie had to pull herself together just to thank him for her surprise.

"Oh, those," he said, "the roses are pretty, but they're not your surprise!"

Is this a fairytale? Katie could hardly believe what was happening to her.

Kurk was the first guy to bring her flowers, the first guy to ever kiss her like that!

He was even saying, 'There's more!" Kurk opened his passenger door while saying, "Get in, madam."

Katie jumped in, asking him, "Where are we going?"

"Oh, you'll see!"

Kurk pulled in front of the Colonial Apartment Complex. "The most modern building in town!" he gloated.

Katie thought to herself, *Marsha, Marsha—Marsha's boyfriend lives here. I wonder which apartment is his?*

Once inside, Kurk had a candlelit dinner catered for them to dine upon. He knew from their conversation that Katie's favorite food was prime rib. So prime rib was the highlight of their meal, with a triple-layered chocolate cake and fresh strawberries on the side as their dessert. Kurk uncorked a bottle of Montepulciano-Di-Abrouzzo, his favorite Italian dry red wine. But Katie insisted on drinking only a sip or two. She drank instead a glass of sweet tea with lemon.

What started out as a scene from a romantic Hollywood movie was about to end as a Morgantown horror flick. The night was soon to reveal that Kurk's intentions was not so innocent after all.

Kurk's overpowering personality mixed with a self-gratifying scheme guaranteed him to be unstoppable. He lured infatuated, naive Katie into his darkened bedroom, and there he raped her. He behaved just like an animal, dismissing Katie's repetitive pleas to *stop*!

"No! Please, Kurk, stop! Don't do this, I'm not that kind of a girl!"

Ignoring her cries, he did his dirty deed and got out of bed.

He said, "I can't believe how traumatized you're acting, Katie. Why, you're just a little country tease, aren't you?"

In disbelief of what just took place, Katie was in shock, thinking, *How could this have happened to me? How could I have been so wrong about Kurk?*

She found her way to his bathroom, and there she sobbed uncontrollably. Kurk opened the door, throwing her panties and jeans onto the bathroom floor.

"Get dressed!" he angrily yelled.

A stunned Katie thought, *What do I do? I want my mommy! ... Think, Katie, just think ... You need to get to your apartment! Get out of his! You're wrong about Kurk, so you don't know what else he's capable of!*

Wisely, Katie pulled herself together and got dressed. She asked Kurk if he would take her home. Remarkably, she handled herself calmly. She needed him to see her demeanor as nonthreatening toward him. After he dropped her off, Katie made her way up her stairs. She opened her front door and locked it behind her.

Sobbing uncontrollably, Katie showered then bathed; then she showered and bathed again. At that point, all she wanted to do was to remove Kurk's smell and his transgression from her body.

The snow had stopped. It no longer looked like much! She took a couple of Tylenol for the pain and went to bed to think and to pray. She was exhausted, violated, and confused.

"How could I have confused such a beast for a gentleman? Why did I laugh Tonie's concerns away? God, why did you let this happen to me?"

Katie fell asleep under the safety of her childhood quilt.

The phone rang, awakening her the next morning at five. Katie was not willing to answer it, so the answering machine picked up the call.

"Katie, it's Tonie. We're going to remain closed until Saturday. Isn't the snow wonderful? It looks just like our powdered sugar, doesn't it? Wish we all had a lot of money, we'd go to Paris for Thanksgiving! Wee, wee!"

"Pray, Katie. Think, Katie. Maybe you should call the police. No! Kurk said he's friends with most of them and that it would only be his word against mine. Should I call Mom? No! She would call the local police department. Should I call Sissy? No! She'd only come here with an attitude, and that would only make things worse!"

Terrified, Katie stayed in her bedroom, with all the doors locked. She forced herself to sleep. Why sleep? Because it was the best alternative to being awake. And maybe, just maybe, if she was lucky, she'd awaken to find out that all this was just a bad dream she was having!

Awake again, Katie took two more Tylenol. Her vagina continued to throb like a bad toothache. Once raped, Katie's body and soul had been invaded by an extreme hypersensitivity to everything.

Twenty-four hours later, Katie was stressed, as no amount of wishful thinking could fix this. None of her mental efforts or spiritual prayers could erase the violation that was done to her.

"It was just supposed to be a spontaneous romantic date!" she cried.

All throughout Katie's teen years, she had longed for a mutual love—one that would sweep her off her feet ... The two would eventually marry, and willingly, on their wedding night, she would give herself to her groom. That was the plan!

But last night wasn't her wedding night...No *I do*'s. No rings. No vows. No white dress. No family gathering. No celebration. She had NO choice!

"Doesn't *NO* still mean NO?"

Katie grieved herself to sleep.

(You got mail!)

> From: Vincent3@aol.com
> To: Katie356@aol.com
>
> I tried to call. No answer. I called the café. Tonie's message says that the café is closed because of snow. Dad and I want to wish you a happy Thanksgiving, honey!! We watched the weather channel and saw that you're getting a dusting

of snow. It's 68 degrees here. Sunny but a little windy. Our neighbors have their grandson and his family down from Maine. They said when they left home they had two feet of snow. The children naturally complained about not being able to play outside in it. So we decided to take them onto the beach and help them make a snowman out of sand. He's complete with a carrot nose and seashell eyes. He looks like he could be *Frosty's* cousin. We named him *Surfy* the sand man. (Get it? Instead of *Surfy* the snowman because he's made of sand.) A little corny, I suppose. But the kids love him! The children even gave him their boogie-board to hold on to. I'm sending you a photo. You should see how many people stop just to take a photo with him!!! One family even told us that their group shot they were taking with *Surfy* was going to be their family Christmas card this year. How do you and Sissy say it?… That's COOL! Your dad & I enjoy watching the red and yellow sunrises here. Yesterday, after sunrise, he took me out for pancakes at the Tropical Pancake House on Orange Beach. They were so delicious. We hope you're staying warm! Remember to wear grandma's scarf and mittens when you go outside. Something else you may find interesting. Down here, your dad and I are considered "*Snow Birds.*" It's a term the locals use for us 55+ that travel south for the warmer weather. They stay the winter then leave the following spring. Makes sense, doesn't it? Migrating birds do it, so why not humans. Dad now calls me his little snow birdie. Isn't he a hoot?

Love you,
Mom and Dad

EMMALEA

From: Sissy4short@aol.com
To Katie356@aol.com

Katie girl,

    Happy Happy Happy Turkey Day!!!! I'm thinking about hopping on the Amtrak to celebrate New Year's with you. I need to spend some time with my best bud! And while we're at it, you can show me ISU and what all the fuss is about! Got a lot to Ketchup on.
    Ha Ha!

                                         Sissy

From: KurktheISU@aol.com
To: Katie356@aol.com

    I know now that we are not suited for one another. I hope we can at least be friends. I wanted to let you know that I'll never bother you at work, call you, or come by your place in the future.

                                         Kurk

"He's got the nerve! He should be in jail! He doesn't have the right to e-mail me! Friends don't rape! However, we do have one thing that we both can agree upon. I, too, plan on never talking or seeing him again!"
    Therefore, Katie chose not to reply to his absurd message. Instead she escaped to a bathtub full of lavender bubbles (to do some serious soaking and thinking).
    "How will I ever be able to trust another man? Will I be able to enjoy a loving relationship with my husband on our wedding night?

Will the appearance of fresh fallen snow, red roses, and prime rib continue to haunt me? Can I make a mocha latte and a chicken parm without the terror being attached? *And* that political poster of his needs torn to bits! I'm so glad that the citizens of Morgantown had discernment enough *not* to trust such a monster with their government!

"In a crisis, my mom and dad always told me they'd be there for me. In a crisis, Pastor James said I should pray, also that Jesus cares and that he's always there with me. In a crisis, Mrs. Kline, my psych professor, says I have two choices. I could choose to either *respond or to react*!"

Respond—to react in a way that shows some action.

React—to change or behave in a particular way when something happens, is said, etc.

Katie once again became mentally exhausted and was unable to think any more. She simply cried out for God's help in this, her time of need. After her plea…for the first time in a couple of days, she felt hungry. Katie made herself a piece of peanut butter toast and sipped on a cup of English breakfast tea, with honey and lemon.

The pain in her vagina was easing up some, but the intense pain in her heart had not. She slept on and off again, but by that night's end, Katie had made her decision. She was going to hide being raped under a protective shield of silence. As she was making up her mind, she remembered Reverend James's teaching on forgiveness.

He said, "If we choose not to forgive an offense, then the perpetrator of that offense continues to win! Control can only be regained by giving the offense their marching orders, when forgiveness is applied."

Katie asked herself, "Do I still believe in God? That's an easy one—of course I do! Did I believe that Reverend James taught God's truth? Yes, I believe he did. In fact, Reverend James was instrumental in cultivating my strong belief in God."

Out of all the choices Katie could have made—her parents' way, her psych professor's way to respond or to react, or Reverend James's way—she chose Reverend James's way through her crisis …

She chose to forgive and to continue believing that Jesus still cared for her.

Katie's more determined now than ever to survive this rape. Over the last few days, however, she had wanted to retreat home, just to run away! But she could not because there was no home for her to run to. She could have just showed up at Gulf Shores, but her heart was so heavy her VW wouldn't have been able to carry it! Katie decided instead to rest and recover in Morgantown. In time, she believed that she'd have enough strength to return to both school and to work at the café.

And by forgiving Kurk, his boundaries were frozen in time and *could not* control her future. Katie's biggest torment now was what her parents would think if they were to ever find out. Both of her parents had sheltered her from evil her entire life. She had to plead with them repeatedly just to allow her to travel to Indiana to go to school. She pleaded her case successfully by reassuring them that she could take care of herself.

But I lied to them, Katie thought. *I didn't take good care of myself! I have to see to it that they never find out, for it would crush them both.*

"No more struggling, this mind battle is over! I, Katie, WIN! Kurk, the smooth monster, LOSES! It was not my fault!"

Yet Katie continued to grieve all that weekend. The focus of her grief had changed; it was solely for the loss of her virginity.

On Monday Katie regained some balance in her life, just enough to return to work and school. Both she had enjoyed immensely. From her time of decision, anytime Kurk and his dreadful act tried to force its way into her thought life, Katie would sing, read out loud, read scripture, or call someone. Katie had the knowledge that it was a proven fact that when we talk, our thoughts stop to listen. (*Try it, you'll see it's true!*)

She handled life one day at a time. Classes were still manageable just by showing up, taking notes, and completing the assigned papers and turning them into her professors for the credit. Work was manageable also. Punch in, take the orders, fill the orders, make the lattes, make the specialty teas, make the coffees and the cappuccinos. Then punch out, go home, eat a little something, do a little cleaning, do a little laundry, prep for the next day's classes, pray, then sleep some.

After the first week, Katie realized her new life of secrecy was working. She knew a little about keeping secrets—secrets not of this magnitude but secrets nonetheless. Katie had Sissy to thank for that! Sissy also taught her how to keep them too. Like the one when Sissy broke her mother's new bottle of expensive cologne. Sissy told her mother that Tiger, their tabby cat, knocked it over, breaking it on the powder room floor.

Katie told Sissy, "It wasn't your cat's fault!"

Sissy replied, "*Shh, shh!* It's our little secret! Don't you dare tell anyone!"

Another time was when Sissy told her mother that she put the dent in her new car when it was Austin that drove his ten-speed bike into the side of it.

Again Sissy told Katie, "*Shh, shh!* It's our little secret! Don't you dare tell anyone!"

So Katie just shushed!

Katie was managing work and school but chose not to go back to church. Instead she spent her Sundays off resting. After all, she was not in a rock-'n-roll celebratory mood quite yet.

Through it all, Katie did remain a compassionate soul. There was an older lady searching for some change to have enough to pay for her meal at the café. Katie stopped her search as she took the $5.79 out of her tip jar and put it in the café's cash register, covering it.

And with every tender act of kindness given, Katie felt a healing come to her heart. Realizing this, she found herself searching for more and more opportunities to present themselves—like escorting a freshman who needed to find her way to her next class, like sharing a meal with a homeless person, like painting the bathroom in her loft apartment without asking for compensation from her landlord.

Mrs. James had always told the WCBC youth group, "No act of kindness, big or small, goes unnoticed by God," and Katie believed her.

Katie began to feel stronger and was well on her way back to a somewhat safer and more secure place. Still it wasn't enough for Tonie. She knew the carefree, lighthearted Katie before Thanksgiving and the Katie after. Something was out of place. Something was just not right!

(You got mail!)

> From: Vincent3@aol.com
> To: Katie356@aol.com
>
> I am so glad to hear that Sissy is coming for New Year's. Did you have fun with Kurk's family over the holidays?
>
> Love
> Mom

Katie thought it was easier for them to assume that she spent the holidays with Kurk than for her to make excuses why she could not come to the Gulf.

(Reply.)

> From: Katie356@aol.com
> To: Vincent3@aol.com
>
> Christmas here was fun. The Gingerbread Café's party was catered. Tonie ordered sushi, moo-goo-guy pan, fried rice, shrimp eggrolls, and we exchanged gifts. I got Jo Ann's name and she got mine. She gave me a gift card to Victoria Secret's. Concerning Kurk, we both decided to stop seeing each other. We just want different things out of life. Thanks for the new cookware set! I'll send Grandma and Grandpa a note thanking them for the money to get my next oil change done. Every little bit helps! Missing you

both and Clarion too. You and Daddy are the greatest!

> Love,
> Katie

From: Sissy4short@aol.com
To: Katie356@aol.com

Coming on the 29th. Meet me at the Amtrak station at 2pm. I'll be the one with the purple and black polka dot oversized suitcase. Just in case you've forgotten what I look like!

> Lotsa love,
> Sissy

(Reply.)

From: Katie356@aol.com
To: Sissy4short@aol.com

I'll be the only one driving a vintage-green Super Bug that has a supersized hug just for you. Back at cha!

> Katie

It had been several weeks since Katie would allow herself to enjoy anything much. But now she was looking forward to enjoying a visit from her very best friend in the whole wide world! A good long talk under a comfy, cozy, crazy quilt was just the thing they both had need of.

(You got mail!)

From: Vincent3@aol.com
To: Katie356@aol.com

So sorry, honey, to hear about you and Kurk. If you're OK? You are OK, aren't you? By the way, I did remember to tell Grandpa that you said the juniors and seniors there are stressed over paying back their student loans and that he was right concerning them. He says he knows you're on your own and it's been more expensive than you thought. I reassured him that your hard work is keeping you debt-free. The family is so very proud of you. Dad says if you're ever in need of a little extra money, just let him know. And he can dig a little deeper into his trouser pockets.

XOXO
Mom and Dad

There she was!

"Sissy, just look at you! You look all grown-up! Where's the blue hair?"

"Katie girl, you look so refined! What's with that stylish short hair? I thought you said you gained ten pounds?"

"Well, actually, I gained thirteen, recently I lost all but one pound of it. Remember how we used to be able to eat everything… all day long and not gain a pound?"

Sissy laughed, answering, "Yep, I do! When I first started working at the Freeze, I ate up most of my paycheck, but now I can't stand the stuff we sell there."

"Austin! Where did you come from? You came too?"

Katie wasn't upset, just somewhat surprised! He startled her as he stepped off the train, with a small brown duffel bag in one hand and a very large purple-and-black polka-dot suitcase around the other! Katie pointed at his load, and Sissy joked, as they both burst into muffled laughter.

"Come on, little brother, group hug."

Austin gladly dropped his load and did as Sissy said. (*Again!*)

This was the first hug Katie had received or had given since…It felt more than awkward for her, to say the least.

"Katie, I hope you don't mind me tagging along. I guess something's never change!" Austin said with an adorable grin on his face. "I've been talking with Belinda Hardesty, Bucky Steven's cousin. Have you had a chance to meet up with her yet?"

"No, ISU is a very big place."

"That's okay, you're going to get your chance. She's invited all of us to her New Year's Eve party. That is, if you don't already have plans?"

"Now, Austin Tatterson, I don't think you traveled over seven hundred miles by train, expecting me to say that I have plans. Sissy and I both will go with you to your friend's party."

Sissy rolled her eyes as she nudged Katie's arm, saying, "He needs us for moral support. This sure is just like old times, isn't it?"

Katie hoped Austin hadn't noticed her staring at him. He sure had changed. He used to be a skinny, pimple-faced, needy boy just a little over four years ago. Time appeared to have taken care of all that! Another improvement that Katie had noticed throughout their stay with her was that he no longer lived in the shadow of his deceased older brother. Not once did he even mention Corey. It used to be every other sentence was about Corey—how Corey would do this, what Corey would say, what Corey wouldn't say. He also got rid of those heavy black geeky glasses and now wore contact lenses. His eyes were blue, who knew, and his hair…

"Katie. Katie girl!" Sissy yelled. "Where is that green bug of yours parked? No one has squashed it yet, I hope!"

Arriving at Katie's apartment, Sissy insisted on Austin paying for a pizza delivery, and he did as Sissy said. Katie made the group root beer floats to have with their pizza and her homemade cherry chocolate chip cookies for dessert.

That evening stretched well into the night as those three talked about almost every childhood story they could remember. They laughed so hard at the one when the girls went to their very first

Mary Kay party. There Katie put lipstick on as eye shadow, and Sissy put eye shadow on as lipstick! (Sissy had almost forgotten about that one.) She laughed so hard that Sissy peed her pants. She ran into the bathroom still laughing!

Katie took advantage of her accident to make Austin a comfortable place to sleep on her pink-striped sofa. Katie had been desiring that she and Sissy would have some alone time together. So while Austin was taking a shower, those two best friends got on their pj's. Then they went into the kitchen, pillaging the rest of the pizza and a few more cookies. With two tall glasses of milk on a serving tray, they headed off to bed.

Katie's queen-size brass bed was comfortably made with an apricot and yellow patchwork quilt, one she had purchase at her local JC Penney's red-tag sale. At those prices, she could purchase six matching floral pillows. Sissy couldn't help noticing and joking that her bed just fit into her tiny bedroom!

Sissy sat down on the bed and could not hold it in any longer! She erupted like a volcano—telling Katie about her feelings for Reverend Wade. As Sissy went on and on, Katie admired her sweet, girly emotions, even to the point that hearing them ignited within Katie a longing for a guy to call her own.

"Katie, I just know you'd like him and approve of him. He's eight years older than me, but that doesn't really matter, does it?"

"No, not if you really love him and he really loves you."

"I thought so! Let me tell you a little bit about him. He attended seminary in Tennessee. After that, his first job was as a youth pastor in Cleveland, Tennessee. Reverend James and God asked him to pray about Clarion, Alabama. He came to Clarion to explore what an amazing opportunity he would have there, as Reverend James's said he would…And that was that! He's now in the deep South, and I have God and Reverend James to thank for that! Why, even Mrs. Betts says, 'What a fine job he is doing at WCBC!' You and I both know that it's not easy to please Mrs. Betts!"

Sissy rambled on and on for at least another hour.

"Before retiring, Reverend James asked if I would help Wade."

"Oh, it's Wade now, is it?"

"That I would help Reverend Wade after he was gone, and I have Austin in on it too! He's been helping me out by showing 'Reverend Wade' around the church's new computer system. Austin even updated the printer and installed a fax machine."

"Welcome to the twenty-first-century Clarion, Alabama!"

"Oh, Katie, I think I love him, and I think he likes me."

"Now, Sissy, take your time. Don't be alone with him. Make sure someone else is always around. You really don't know a lot about him yet, now, do you?"

"Okay, Miss Gloomy-Gus, I won't be in any hurry. I promise I'll be careful. I remember all those lectures our mothers gave us."

"Listen…I'm serious about this, Sissy! Both of our mothers were telling us the truth!"

"Okay, okay, I promise."

"I can't eat another bite. I can't talk or hear another sentence," Katie said. "Just give me a hug, and let's say our prayers…Amen! I love you, Sissy."

"I love you, Katie girl."

"I'm sure glad you came and Austin too. But he's not the boy that I remembered."

Austin heard his name mentioned and Katie's comment. That brought a smile to his face.

He interrupted, saying, "Hey, you two in there, do you know what time it is?"

"Okay, okay," they both said in unison. "See you in the morning."

"Girls, *it is* morning!"

Like the little girls they once were, they giggled their way to sleepy town, as they used to call it.

Austin tossed and turned. *Bam! Boom! Crash!* "Austin, what are you doing in there?"

"Sis, I can't sleep, so I am trying to make us some coffee."

Katie yelled at him, "Forget about it. Give us a few minutes to get dressed, and I'll take you both to a place where you'll be served the best cup of coffee in the entire state of Indiana."

(You may have already guessed it.) They were going to the Gingerbread Café.

The girls ordered a double expresso each. Austin ordered a large latte with a shot of caramel. Katie was proud to be able to introduce them both to Tonie and to Jo Ann. Tonie and Jo Ann were surprised to see Austin. Katie did not tell them that he was coming. Besides, the way Katie had described him, they thought he was a little boy.

Also they both were under the impression that he was homely-looking and a real nuisance. This young man standing before them was quite a *cutie-patootie*! He certainly was funny and attached to these two in very different ways. With Sissy, he interjected into the conversation, only when she allowed him too. As for Katie, they noticed he probably liked her more than just as a hometown friend. Those two girls could not see any of it because they were too deep into their reminiscing to notice.

Jo Ann asked, "Austin, have you had to listen to this chatter all night long?"

"Yes, ma'am, I sure have. Ever since we got off the train yesterday afternoon."

"For that, young man, you deserve an award. I'm going to make you another latte on the house!"

Tonie chimed in, "And here, have a gingerbread '*man*' cookie too! Now it's two girls and two guys. You're no longer outnumbered."

The four of them walked toward ISU. Katie proudly toured them around her university. She introduced them as being her friends from back home. *Back home*…Just saying those words tasted sweeter to Katie than any dessert she had eaten lately. She knew God had sent them to her at this very specific time in her life. And she planned on enjoying every minute that they were together.

They hung out at Morgantown's new mall, The Rivers Edge. Austin requested that Katie take him to her favorite grocery store, going in alone and telling them he'd be right back. He purchased the food items that he needed to make his famous chili-con-carney and his double-cheese grilled cheese toast on French bread.

Taking the dishes to the sink, Sissy complimented Austin.

"Little bro, that was tasty. Where did you learn to cook like that?" Taking the opportunity, she rubbed the top of his head, saying, "Did *a girrrl* teach you?"

"No, but when you're out on your own, you learn to do a lot of new things just to survive. Isn't that right, Katie?"

Katie answered with heavy eyes, "We sure do!"

Austin noticed that Katie was about to nod off, so he stood to his feet, announcing, "Tonight it's Austin's rule. And if anyone objects with my rule, they must do the dishes and clean up my kitchen mess."

Looking at the huge kitchen mess, the girls begged for him to tell them his rule!

"*My* rule is that lights are out in five minutes, because tomorrow's New Year's Eve and all of us need to sleep tonight!"

"And the clock starts *now*!"

Katie looked at Sissy. Sissy looked at Katie. They both jumped up and ran into her tiny bedroom. They hopped into Katie's bed… clothes on and all.

"And no talking or whispering in there!"

Giggling they answered him sarcastically…"*Yesss*, Poppa Austin!"

"Good night!" he strongly replied. "And don't make me have to come in there, you two!"

Katie jokingly asked, "When you're done in the kitchen, can you clean the bathroom too? I gave my maid a couple days off."

He ran in and flipped a dishcloth at her, saying, "I don't think so! Good night, children!"

"Good night, Austin, we love you. You're our hero!"

He reached to turn off the bedroom light, saying, "I love you too, now get some sleep!"

They whispered, "He sure sounds like our dads, doesn't he?"

"He sure does!"

The next morning the girls were awakened by a phone conversation Austin was having with Belinda (they assumed).

"Shh," Sissy said. "Let's listen, we might hear something we can use against the kid later."

Katie didn't like to eavesdrop; however, she willingly listened in as Sissy had suggested.

"Yes," said Austin. "We can be there around five o'clock. And after dinner, we'll help you set up for the party. Oh, I'm sure they won't mind. They both work in food service and are really good at it."

They lounged around until one thirty snacking and watching a couple of movies on her DVD player, *Mrs. Doubtfire* and *Fire Down Below*. Austin rented them both from Blockbuster Video at the River's Edge mall yesterday.

After the movies...it took the girls three hours to get ready. (*Yes, I said it correctly...three hours!*) Showers, hair, nails, dressing and redressing...when finally, Austin had to take the lead once again by saying, "Girls, you have no time to change again! You both look fantastic. Remember, Belinda wants us to come for dinner at five."

They submitted and ran to Katie's bug. Once belted in, Katie asked Austin for the directions to Belinda's place.

"Belinda said you should know how to get there. She lives in town at the Colonial Apartment Complex in building number 3, apartment C. Are you familiar with the place? If you're not...I can call her for the directions."

Katie wanted to run back inside to hide out. She fought back a tear from falling. She appeared to be spaced out, as if she was going into shock. Both Austin and Sissy became somewhat alarmed—especially since she was just so full of fun and looking forward to the hopes of having some New Year's jubilation. Now she looked so fragile-looking.

"Katie...Katie girl...are you okay?"

"I'm...I'm just fine."

Katie knew if she cried, her secret would be out, and she could not risk that.

"We'll be there in fifteen minutes. Do you guys want to listen to John Denver?"

Katie popped in his Christmas cassette. She sang along with John, and they joined in too.

Sissy says, "It's the holidays, a girl can be a little melancholy, can't she?"

"Austin, did you say building number 3?"

They arrived right on time. Belinda made her signature salmon dinner. No doubt to impress them and she did just that. Her meal tasted like it came from a five-star restaurant. Belinda was the whole package. She's beautiful, intelligent, and an amateur chef too. She would graduate summa cum laude from ISU and was the senior class president.

Katie thought, *What's up with Colonial Apartments? Is it entirely full of aspiring politicians?*

After dinner they were joined by two other friends of Belinda's. The six of them speedily set up a black-and-gold themed New Year's Eve Party. It was one that reviled *any* ritzy New Year's event at *any* New York venue. Her celebration planning was complete with savory and sweet hors-d'oeuvres, chilled champagne, and sparkling cider too.

Guests started arriving a little before ten. In walked Kurk, with Marsha, Marsha, Marsha!

So he was the boyfriend! Marsha had managed to maintain her appearance of perfection on the outside.

I guess to Kurk, that's really what matters the most. It's not our major organ, known as the heart, especially since he dismisses other people's feelings as if they don't matter at all!

It's too late. Marsha saw Katie as she went for the kitchen to regroup. Seizing the opportunity, Marsha slithered her way over to show off the 2-carat solitaire engagement ring that Kurk gave her earlier that day.

Marsha *boastfully* said, "Daddy said that we could get married in June at his country club and that only the famous and the elite would be attending."

Sissy spoke up and said, "I guess that counts us out now, doesn't it, Katie girl?"

Marsha introduced Kurk to Katie.

"Hello, Katie." Kurk asked. "Who's your friends?"

"They both are really good friends of mine from home."

Austin spoke up, "Belinda's my friend. She invited us to ring in the New Year with her."

Sissy spoke up, "A New Year always brings with it a *lotta* new possibilities, doesn't it, Katie?"

It was obvious that Sissy didn't like either Kurk or Marsha, since they both looked down upon them as if they were royalty and the three of them were mere peasants. Sissy saw right through them too ... They both were just *a couple of wannabes*!

"Ten, nine, eight, seven, six, five, four, three, two, one...Happy New Year!"

Noise makers everywhere and *Auld langsyne* was being sung. There was even a firework display over the Morgantown's city stadium skyline.

Belinda kissed Austin. All night long it was easy to see that she was fond of him. Marsha kissed Kurk.

"Gross, get a room!" Sissy said. Sissy had always been known to be ready to pick a fight.

Thank God, her cell phone rang. It was Pastor Wade calling to wish her a Happy New Year. Also he wanted to let her know that his cat, Wendy, had four kittens and that he wanted to give her the one of her choice.

After describing them to her, Sissy said, "I want the snow-white one with the pink nose. I'll call her Snowball!"

Katie felt invisible. She glanced over at Kurk and Marsha, thinking, *Well, those two deserve each other.*

Then she looked at Austin in disbelief. *He's a man now! And he's with a beautiful lady that's been flirting with him all night long! Imagine that. I just have never seen him that way!*

Sissy ran over and gave Katie a kiss and a huge Happy New Year's hug. Kurk and Marsha left, having a few other parties to attend (to show off her rock...no doubt about it!), while all others snapped photos and helped clean up the mess. Austin, Katie, and Sissy returned to Katie's apartment around 5:00 a.m.

Katie moaned, saying, "I'm not feeling too good, my stomach's a little upset. I think I ate too much. My appetite isn't what it used to be you know. Seeing all that fancy food, I just couldn't resist. Stuffed mushrooms, smoked salmon, asparagus wrapped in bacon, and all the shrimp I could eat. Not to mention all of those delicious dessert bites."

Sissy said, "Katie girl, you just overdid it, that's all. We Tattersons are scheduled to take the 9:00 a.m. train today. I know, it's New Year's Day, but we must go because Austin must finish a paper that's due this Wednesday and I need to reopen the Freeze tomorrow morning. However, before we go, I'm personally making you a cup of peppermint tea, just like your grandma use to make for us. Remember the time when we ate too much cotton candy and all those corn dogs at the Fourth of July celebration in our freshman year? Today I still refuse to eat a single bite of a corn dog! And thank God we don't sell them at the Freeze…If we did, I'd have to resign. Wait a minute, I can't, I'm the owner! You go get in bed, and Austin and I will take a taxicab to the station."

Katie spoke up, "No way! I'm going to take you both to catch the train!"

Austin pushed back, saying, "No, you will not. You get your rest. We'll be just fine!"

Katie awakened to an empty apartment. There was a note on her desk that read,

Katie,

>We left without kisses and hugs, just in case you got the flu BUG! Hey, Katie girl, what's up with you and BUGS anyway? Ha, ha, ha! Thanks for your hospitality!

>Love,
>Sissy & I guess…Austin too

Before boarding the train, Austin called Tonie to inform her that Katie was not feeling well, asking her to please check in on her a little later. He gave her his contact information, just in case Katie should ever need anything.

Silence. "I sure miss them already. Their visit was way too short, but sweet enough, I guess."

Katie then checked her e-mail account.

(You got mail!)

> From: KurktheISU@aol.com
> To: Katie356@aol.com
>
> Katie, thanks for not saying anything last night. I need to give you a heads-up. Marsha plans on coming by the café tomorrow for brunch, before heading back to the city. Belinda's party was OK. It would have been more successful if she would've had a better selection of booze!
>
> Kurk

"What a jerk! I guess I'm supposed to be grateful that they'll grace me with their presence tomorrow? *No, that's not it.* He's afraid that I'll not keep my composure, exposing his dirty deed! Well, he doesn't have to worry. I'll keep it in hiding. But I won't be doing it for him, it's for me and my well-being. I'm managing just fine now, and I refuse to let him destroy the peace that's been restored in my life."

It had taken Katie several weeks for her fortress to be refortified to the place where Kurk was unable to harm her anymore.

"I will serve them professionally with a smile, and hopefully that will be the last time I'll ever have to see them both!"

Katie ate a small supper and kept it down.

It appears all is well. It must have been Belinda's rich food after all!

Katie had *no* elevated temperature and *no* chills, so she automatically ruled out having the flu. She was thankful that it appeared not to be the flu because it had been going around campus for a couple of weeks now.

The following morning, Katie awakened having to run to the bathroom where she vomited again. As she went to stand, the bathroom spun. She crawled back into bed and called off work. She also contacted a fellow classmate, Trudy Davis, that had four of the same classes that she did. Trudy said that she'd e-mail Katie all missed assignments, especially in pharmacology class. Katie knew if she missed a single day in Mrs. Goins's pharmacology class, it would be almost impossible to recover. The rest was not a problem. For they were easily made up. She slept until 4:00 p.m.

(You got mail!)

> From: Vincent3@aol.com
> To: Katie356@aol.com
>
> How was your time with Sissy? I heard it through the grapevine that Austin came too. Did you kids have a good time talking about the good ole days? Just wanted to let you know that dad has lost fifteen pounds to my five pounds. Mainly because we are walking on the beach three miles a day. Dad told me this morning, he's thinking about going deep-sea fishing this afternoon. There is a fishing boat that he can charter in Fairhope. You're always asking about what I am doing. You'll be glad to know that I've started writing a cookbook. Aunt Eldee has already caught wind of it. She wants to be the very first person to purchase a copy. (*I wonder why?*) I was wondering, can I put your lemon-brownie recipe in it? Your dad and I have enjoyed our stay here. Our condo is comfortable enough, and we have all we have need of. However, we sure miss being around people our own age. We've enjoyed being around a much older population, but you know us, we relate better to younger adults more around our age group because *we're still very young at heart.* We have enjoyed meeting the other *Snow Birds,* listening to their life stories. Most meetings came from the many conversations we shared during our walks on the beach and then joining them over a dinner at one of the shore's many restaurant choices. While this

experience has been a *pleasant one,* we long for *home*!! Keep us in your prayers. Join us in asking God *"Where do we go from here?"* We will recommend to everyone Gulf Shores, as it is a very nice place to visit when you need some *"vitamin SEA."* (Ha, ha, ha, GET IT!) Speaking of home, the local TV and radio stations down here sure do give the song *Sweet Home Alabama* a lot of playtime!

Love,
Mom

(Reply.)

From: Katie356@aol.com
To: Vincent3@aol.com

Mom, we did have a lot of fun!! But we're not little kids anymore. But I know we'll always be kids to you and Dad. It's OK to use my recipe. However, before doing so, make sure to get a promise from Aunt Eldee that she'll not sell them in her pastry shop, because Sissy still sells them at the Freeze. Glad you're having fun because you and Daddy deserve it! Sounds like the beach will NOT be your new home. God will guide you guys to a home just like he always has.

Xoxo
Katie

P.S. Austin came too. He sure has grown up! AND Sissy's in love!

From: KurktheISU@aol.com
To: Katie356@aol.com

> Marsha asked about you today, when we ate at the café. They said "You were home sick." Jo Ann was making you some homemade chicken noodle soup. She was planning on bringing it over after closing. Marsha insisted that we bring it by, on our way to the airport around five. I did everything I could to stop her, but you know Marsha, she always gets her way! Don't tell her about us. I mean, nothing about us! Thanks for calling Tonie, telling her staff not to mention us dating.
>
> Kurk

Before Katie had a chance to reply, the doorbell rang. *Dingdong!*
Katie looked out her living room window and saw Kurk's car parked out in front. She slipped on her robe and opened the door.
Marsha rushed in, saying, "Jo Ann made you this soup. I volunteered to bring it to you, since your apartment is on my way to the airport! I know I may have not been the friendliest toward you in the past, but I'm hoping this will make amends for that." She handed her the café's takeout bag with Jo Ann's aromatic soup inside.
The odor from the chicken noodle soup caused Katie to excuse herself to go to the bathroom, where she vomited again. Marsha, being Marsha, invaded Katie's privacy. She walked over to the computer screen and read what was on Katie's screen.
There was an e-mail from Kurk!
After reading it, Marsha took it upon herself to reply to Kurk. (Reply.)

From: Katie356@aol.com
To: KurkISU@aol.com

Honey, I'm here! Katie's in the bathroom. Since she didn't reply, **I AM!** Aren't you the slick one! You get only one bad decision in our relationship, **AND THIS ONE IS IT!** I'm going to say this only once, and I will never say it again! **THERE WILL NEVER BE A SECOND! AND** If there is, you will force me to tell **DADDY!** Here's what you are going to do next. Go to the "More Actions" heading and click "Filter Messages like these." Blocking all future messages from Katie356@aol.com. **DO IT NOW!** Then you're going to give your 30-day notice at work and sublease your apartment. Then you'll move to New York to be with me. Don't worry, I'll talk to Daddy. We'll move up our wedding date to a Valentine's Day wedding, saying that we cannot wait to start our new life together. From there I'll make it all happen. <u>***We will never talk about this ever again***</u>, **GOT IT!**

Your fiancée—Marsha

She clicked the *send* button and turned off the computer, before running out the front door.

Katie came out of the bathroom to find Marsha gone.

"That's strange, Marsha's gone and my computer's turned off!"

Looking out the window, she saw that Kurk's car was gone too. Relieved, Katie sat on her couch and began to watch *Friends* on TV. She ate a cup of Jo Ann's soup, and surprisingly, it stayed down. Katie called Jo Ann to thank her. Then she talked with Tonie, letting her know that she'd be at work tomorrow after her third class.

She also told Tonie, "I'll never eat smoked salmon again!"

Checking the messages on her voice mail, Katie heard Sissy's message, letting her know that they both had arrived home and that they had a lot of fun.

Katie called Sissy back and had to leave a message on her voice mail, saying, "I'm feeling much better, and I plan on going back to school and work tomorrow."

Katie said her prayers and went to bed early. She even thanked God that Marsha and Kurk were no longer entangled in her life and that she was free to focus her emotional energy elsewhere.

"Amen!"

Morning came, and the nausea and vomiting returned. Katie slept in, missing all three classes. She felt better by two o'clock, so she went into work as promised. The café staff noticed that Katie looked peaked. At the end of her shift, Tonie called Katie into her office so the two of them could talk privately. Katie knew she had complied with company policy regarding calling off work.

So she thought, *What could be the problem? I know I'm a little tired, but I completed all my customers' orders with* no complaints.

"Straight up! Katie, are you pregnant?"

"Absolutely not! Why would you ask me that?"

"The signs!"

"What signs?"

"Morning sickness. You're studying on becoming a nurse, you tell me what they are … Here!" Tonie handed her a Rite Aid bag. Then Tonie left her office to go make a fresh pot of decaf coffee that Jo Ann was requesting.

Katie opened the bag. Inside was a home pregnancy test kit. Katie clocked out, taking the bag with her, as she quickly went home. She read the instructions and went to the bathroom to pee on the stick.

A red plus sign (+ … *positive*) presented itself.

Chapter Seven

Now What?

"*Now what...do I do?*" Katie cried.

Positive and *plus* were two words that in any other circumstance would have brought Katie joy—*a tiny bundle of joy*, that is.

"But how did Tonie know? Tonie knows! What does she know? What does she presume to know? What does she think of me now?"

She screamed, "I'm pregnant! It can't be! Dear God, this is more than I can bear!"

The doorbell rang. Katie hoped that whoever it was outside of her door didn't hear her ranting.

She wasn't expecting anyone. She wasn't expecting any deliveries. Katie tiptoed to her door and peeked through her peephole. It was Tonie! Katie was much too embarrassed to answer. Tonie rang the doorbell four more times before she finally gave up and left.

Katie watched from the living room window to make sure that she did. There she saw the strangest thing. Tonie placed a note under her VW's wiper blade before driving off.

Katie thought, *Why would she do that? What does the note say? Oh my goodness, what if somebody else reads it?*

Shoeless, Katie ran to get that mysterious blue note, finding that it was not a note after all. It was a pamphlet from the South Central Women's Clinic downtown. Katie retreated to her loft, locking the door behind her. She jumped into bed and began to read.

South Central's Women's Clinic provided the following services for the women of Morgantown: health screenings, pap smears, cervical cancer tests, condoms, birth control, mammograms, and abortions.

"*Abortions*! What is Tonie saying? Does she think that I am that kind of a girl? I'm a Christian, and she knows that! What motivated her in coming clear across town just to bring me this pamphlet?"

Katie's phone rang, but she refused to answer it. Tonie left her the following message:

"Katie, I know you're there. I covered your shift for the next two days. I'm coming back over to your place on the third day, and we'll talk then. I want you to know that you're not alone and that you're not the only young lady that has found herself in your predicament. Love ya, sweetie."

Katie saw someone had used her e-mail account to answer Kurk because she knew that she didn't.

"You've got to be kidding me! It was Marsha! Now she knows! I can't believe it! She had the nerve to reply to Kurk's message to me, from my personal computer! The nerve these two have! She told Kurk to block all my e-mails. She doesn't even know the half of it yet…The other half is that…he raped me and the consequences of that unprotected sex is that he got me…pregnant, that's what!"

(You got mail!)

> From: Sissy4short@aol.com
> To: Katie356@aol.com
>
> Last time we talked, I forgot to thank you for sharing your cherry chocolate chip cookie recipe with me. I made them as an early Valentine's gift for Wade. He enjoyed them so much he suggested that I should begin selling them at the Freeze. I did, and they're a hit! I can't seem to bake them fast enough. I guestimate with the profits, I'll be able to afford to

replace the Freeze's front awning next spring. I've been selling them three for a $1, with no complaints. I call them *"KT cookies!"* I thought my best friend would like that! *Do you know her?* You should ... she's a doozy! So I was thinking... The next time you see Austin, I do believe he owes for all the cookies he chocked down when we stayed at your place? I took a few pictures of Wade and me. You'll be getting them in your granny's package that she's mailing out today. Wade and I are an item now here in Clarion. He makes me so happy. He's not at all like those Lumberport boys. Looking back, I really liked Barry's Mustang and Jet Ski's more than I liked him. How lame was that? When you get the picture, you'll see that my Wade is a little round in the middle and a little bald on top. But Katie, he loves me and has captured my whole heart. I truly do love that preacher man. Imagine that? You're the good one, Katie. I always thought that you would end up marrying a preacher, not me! OK, I can hear you saying, "Sissy, has he even asked you yet?" No, he hasn't yet, but I got a notion he's going to! Enough about me. Are you seeing anyone? Any available preachers there in Morgantown? What about that rock-n-roll church, any available preachers there?

xoxo
Sissy

P.S. Mother and Dad asked Austin and I if we want to have an Easter weekend get-together at their new house with our entire family, including yours. What do you think? I believe it would be marvelous, simply marvelous!

Katie talked out loud to herself.

"Preacher's wife! What preacher would want me now? I'm damaged goods. I'm the good one, right! I can't call and talk with Sissy, she won't understand. Easter? A weekend get-together! That's the least of my concerns. I can't think of anything else right now. Anyway, how could I reply to her? I have nothing worth saying!"

On the third day, around six o'clock, Katie's doorbell rang. It was Tonie! This time Katie let her in. Tonie brought dinner for them both, and they began their evening together. They ate without saying a solitary word. Tonie had never seen Katie so hungry and so disheveled. Her hair needed to be combed, and she sure could use a hot shower. After sharing Tonie's lasagna and salad meal, Tonie instructed Katie to go get cleaned up while she did the dishes. Then she'd put the tea kettle on so the two of them could share a cup of jasmine tea.

Expecting some resistance, Katie surprised her by saying, "I would like that."

Tonie quickly did the dishes, tidied the living room area, made up Katie's bed, and gathered all the dirt laundry, placing them in the clothes hamper where they belonged.

A refreshed Katie joined Tonie in the living room.

"Now that's much better," Tonie said with a smile.

Looking around at Tonie's thoughtfulness, Katie let go, falling into Tonie's lap.

Tonie's not her momma, but then again, her momma would never be able to handle this. So in this case, Tonie would just have to do. For three days now, Katie had been struggling deep down in her soul. She had totally isolated herself and had become bitter and was unable to pray. Tonie kept quiet, giving Katie all the space she needed to say what she was feeling.

Eventually, Katie began to speak.

"Tonie, Kurk took my innocence away from me! I've been saving myself for my wedding night! How could I have been so wrong about him? I should have listened to you! You were right about him all along ... Tonie, he raped me, and now I'm pregnant!

"As far back as I can remember, I have dreamed of becoming a mother. When I was a little girl, I had my favorite baby doll. She was so real to me. Her name is Emmalea, and I still have her. She's is in my mother's old cedar chest for safekeeping, back in Alabama. Emmalea and I were inseparable. We'd do everything together, until I got too old to play with her anymore. That's when my mom and I put her away. It's because of her that I daydream about becoming a real mother.

"Back in Clarion, I would share with Sissy my daydreams about getting married. That my husband and I would pick out our baby's names. We would decorate the nursery. We would stroll her in the town park. We'd sing her to sleep, read her the *Velveteen Rabbit*, teach her to play paddy-cake, run outside blowing bubbles into the wind. Her daddy would carry her…bouncing her on his masculine shoulders. Build her a playhouse on the lawn and buy her a puppy to grow up with.

"Kurk was an animal on top of me!"

Katie described the details of his intrusive act to Toni. Then she cried herself to sleep. Tonie gently rocked Katie in her arms, as if she were a baby herself. Twenty-minutes had passed since Katie's last whimper. Tonie saw that Katie had fallen into a deep sleep. She gently laid her head down on a pillow close by. Covering Katie with a blanket, she waited.

Two and a half hours later, Katie awakened to that hot cup of tea that Tonie had promised her earlier.

"Katie, let's talk. You drink your tea, and I'll begin. I'm guessing you chose not to report this to the police, am I right?"

Katie motioned her head up and down, indicating yes.

"You're right. It's not supposed to be like this for you or for any woman. I believe the best for you were the daydreams that you dreamed. Instead, the unthinkable happened, and no little girl ever grew up thinking she'd be raped. *MEN should get that!*

"You asked me months ago why I didn't like Kurk. I told you that I couldn't put my finger on any one thing, that I just knew that he was wrong for you! Sadly, now we both know why.

"I want to share with you a secret of mine. I've had two different Kurk's in my past. The first was a much older man. He took advantage of his teenage babysitter's naivety. He did this by telling her that he loved her, instead of showing her that he did, he dumped her after impregnating her young body.

"You would have thought I would have learned my lesson… But I didn't.

"The second was a dashing young college professor. He promised his student the sun and the moon, if she would only keep their love for one another a secret until his divorce became final. He then would be free to give their unborn love child his last name. There was never ever going to be a divorce, and he never ever intended on being a real father to any child of ours.

"From those two errors in my judgement came two abortions. From those abortions, I found out that *not* all men's promises are kept. After that, I wised up and went on the pill. I remained celibate until I met Neil. Until this very day, I have never told anyone my secret. Not even to my best friend, Jo Ann."

Tonie shed a few tears. Katie handed her a tissue.

Tonie continued, "I have spent the bigger part of my adult life wondering… *What if?* And I don't want that for you. Neil's my true love, my soul mate.

"Together, we've decided not to have any children. We both are very satisfied with our life and work at the café. Unfortunately, those two painful Kurk relationships resulted in me judging myself as less than worthy of ever having a loving relationship. *Thank God, I was wrong*! Neil shows me each day that I am worthy of receiving his love. For his steadfastness, *I am eternally grateful*!

"Katie, I know with all the chaos that you're living with, you can't see it now, but trust me, *true love will come* for you too! Don't ask me how I know. *I just do*! He'll be in your path when you least expect him to be. *He'll be the true promise keeper you need*."

Katie finished her tea and told Tonie that she needed some more rest. Tonie agreed. They didn't even bring up the pregnancy.

"So then, you'll be at work tomorrow?"

Katie answered, "I'm planning on it."

"See you at two," she said as Tonie left quietly.

Two o'clock and no Katie. Tonie went into her office and checked her messages.

There was one from Katie saying, "Hey, Tonie, it's Katie. I need to take care of a few things. I'm needing a couple more days off. I hope to return to work on Friday."

Katie missed her classes, showing no interest in the classwork that she had missed. She worked up enough courage to call and speak with a staff member at the Women's Clinic. She took the rest of the day to decide if she needed to let Kurk know. She tried calling him on his cell phone, but his number had been changed. With no other choice left, she had to e-mail him. Katie knew that she was taking a big risk that Marsha would intercept her message, but it was a chance that she was willing to take.

> From: Katie356@aol.com
> To: KurktheISU@aol.com
>
> I know that Marsha wanted you to block my messages. I hope you have not done so yet. There is one more thing both you and Marsha don't know.
>
> Katie

(*Four hours later!*)
(You got mail!)

> From: KurktheISU@aol.com
> To: Katie356@aol.com
>
> With moving and the wedding, I've been very busy. I haven't found the time to block your messages. Tell me, what's the one thing?
>
> Kurk

(Reply.)

> From: Katie356@gmai.com
> To KurkISU@aol.com
>
> I have been debating on whether I should contact you or not for a couple of weeks now. I believe…you need to know that I'm pregnant.

(Kurk's reply.)

> Whose is IT? The boy at Belinda's New Year's Eve Party?

(Katie's reply.)

> No, if IT was, we wouldn't be having this conversation now, would we? Besides, he never would have violated me the way you did! To answer your question, IT's yours.

(Kurk's reply.)

> How could it be mine? You mean to tell me that you weren't on the pill?

(Katie's reply.)

> Me, on the pill? Why would I be?

(Kurk's reply.)

> You're kidding me, right? What were you thinking? You're in college, and you're not on the pill. Were you trying to trap a guy?

(Katie's reply.)

Clearly, I was NOT thinking correctly when it came to you. The farthest thing from my mind was that you were capable of rape.

(Kurk's reply.)

I can't believe it. This is a mess that I just don't need right now!

(Katie's reply.)

You're upset with me? You've got the nerve! You forced yourself on me, remember?

(Kurk's reply.)

How much is this going to cost me? How much do you need to take care of IT? If you think for one minute I'll give up Marsha and her family's connections just to play daddy, you have another thing coming. Me, marry you? Ha! Why, you're just a country bumpkin from who-knows-where Alabama. And you claim to be a Christian? You're trying to mess up all our lives! I'm running for congressman next year, in the great State of New York. Now you choose to tell me about your problem? Here's the solution…Just get rid of IT!

            Kurk

Up until now, Katie had remained silent. Today, however, she found her voice.

"He says *it's* my problem! My decision! Even after what he had done! I had been kind of hoping that we might marry and that love would follow so that we could raise our baby together. Love being highly overrated, I would just have to *settle* for less. There's that word *settle* again! Why does that word anger me so? I don't have to *settle* for whatever Kurk Levathian decides I deserve! Besides, Tonie encouraged me by saying that eventually my true love will come. *After all…she was right about Kurk…she could be right about that too!*"

Hope once again came to Katie. With it she had a chance for a happy ever after in her future. With hope, despair exits out the back door. After their last e-mail conversation, Katie saw Kurk for the insecure pathetic man that he was. He was only using Marsha for her father's political ties to the Fourth Congressional District. She saw through his charm that once had her blinded to his arrogant, self-absorbed true self. He was not the kind of person that she desired to have connected to her life in any way! With this new revelation, Katie was ready to make her final reply to Kurk Levathian.

> From: Katie356@aol.com
> To: KurktheISU@aol.com
>
> You're under no obligation here. I have money. I do want to thank you for helping me decide what I must do next. I once had hoped… Well, never mind that's water under the bridge, as my country bumpkin father would say! I don't know what I was thinking by contacting you. I'll handle IT. Good-bye!
>
> Katie

Immediately, Katie blocked Kurk from ever being able to contact her again! Then she went and sat on her cozy living room sofa to think.

"The clinic calls *it* an *it*. Kurk calls *it* an *it*. He doesn't want *it*. My family won't accept *it*. I can't handle *it*. This is not the way my parents would like to become grandparents. Furthermore, they don't deserve *it*. Katie…you just need to do *it*…Just go and get *it* over with."

Katie reached for her phone and calls the Women's Clinic. They had a three-o'clock opening today so she took the appointment. She pulled into the clinic's parking lot, which was located right across from the new shopping mall. Passing by it many times before, she always thought it was a doctor's office building.

Today, however, along the sidewalk, there were protesters gathered together. One protestor was yelling out, "Murderer!" She quickly ran into the building's foyer and was relieved to see that she knew no one inside. She was right; the waiting room looked just like a doctor's office. The receptionist handed her a clipboard to fill out all the necessary paperwork and, of course, the payment criteria.

She had several health questions that she needed to answer. She checked the *no box*, saying that she was not on the pill, and the *no box* on that her periods have not been regular. She waited while reading an old copy of a *Good Housekeeping Magazine*.

The clock on the wall said, *Tick-tock, tick-tock, tick-tock.*

After her exam, she was assigned a return visit at nine o'clock tomorrow morning. Katie was relieved that the protesters had gone home for the day. Hungry, Katie went through the Buster Burger drive-through for a cheeseburger and a strawberry shortcake shake.

Arriving home, Katie called Tonie.

"Tonie, can you go with me to my appointment in the morning?"

Tonie answered by asking her *two questions*: "Are you sure?" and "Do you think you need to take a few more days? This is a big decision, possibly the biggest one you'll ever make! I know you said no parents and no Sissy. And I promised to respect that, but…"

Katie cut her off by saying, "Both Kurk and I are sure."

That night Katie could hardly sleep. She tossed and turned, wrestling with her pillows as if she were in a WCW wrestling match.

They arrived at the clinic with new protesters congregated there.

One of them appeared to be a priest, complete with his white collar, yelling out, "It's not a fetus, it's a baby! They're telling you lies! Life begins at conception! Please reconsider!"

Tonie rushed Katie quickly inside, asking, "Are you okay?"

"I'm okay."

"It's your choice, Katie. Whatever you choose, you'll have to live with it as part of your past, not them."

Just like she did yesterday, Katie looked around and saw only strangers sitting in the clinic's waiting room. She signed in at the front desk.

Immediately, a staff member came from behind the double doors and called her name, "Katie V.!"

Katie made this difficult decision with her head, by denying her heart from having any say-so.

Katie went in, and a little later she came out. By then the priest was gone. For that fact, Tonie was relieved.

This kid has been through enough!

Tonie had been in Katie's shoes *twice*, so she knew the emotional aftereffects she'd have to deal with. And no amount of words spoken could short-circuit this process. So experienced, Tonie remained *quiet*. However, they did share in a moment of tears—Tonie for her two *what ifs* and Katie for her one *it*.

Tonie dropped Katie off at her front door. Katie asked Tonie not to come up because she said she needed some time alone.

"Don't worry about your job. I'll cover your days! You come back when you're ready."

(Little did Tonie know at that time that Katie would also choose never to return to work at the Gingerbread Café and never to return to her ISU classes.)

Later in life, Katie would describe what she was feeling that day as being "hollow" inside, also that it was not fair that she'd been forced into making such a decision—a decision that no college student should ever have to make.

That night a windstorm went through Morgantown. It knocked off Katie's power, ISU's power, and over thirty thousand of Branch Electric's customers were left without power for the next thirty-seven hours.

Katie lit a candle. That atmosphere reminded her of WCBC's candlelight services that they'd have around the holidays. She was glad that there was no one to talk to and no movie to watch. The silence was soothing to her soul. Just as in times past, when she'd sat in the church pew hearing the soothing tone of her pastor's voice speaking words of faith.

Her power finally came back on, and Katie threw away the milk, lunch meat, and coffee creamer just in case. She made the decision to isolate herself in her apartment for three weeks. Tonie left messages after messages (the thinking-of-you kind). Trudy left messages that she was missed in all her classes. Leroy at Catron's Oil and Lube said that it was time to change the oil and rotate the bug's tires. Both Mom and Sissy said to call them.

Katie did thank God for one thing: *her savings*. She could survive on it for a little while longer.

(You got mail!)

> From: TatinCO@aol.com
> To: Katie356@aol.com
>
> It's been too long since we have talked. Our family is getting together at our new home in Denver, Colorado, over Easter weekend. I know that's a few weeks away, but this kind of an event needs extra planning time. We want you to come, and we hope you can! If you need help with travel arrangements, Ernie said he can help. It will be just like old times. Save the date!
>
> The Tatterson family

> From: Vincent3@aol.com
> To: Katie356@aol.com
>
> We're back in Alabama. Our trip to Florida was lovely. It seems like it's been forever since we've had a good long talk with each other. We understand that both school and the café have

been keeping you busy. Dad did get in some deep-sea fishing while we were there. He didn't like it much. It was the rocking of the boat that changed his opinion. We both have a nice tan. We also have had our fill of Gulf shrimp. Did you hear from the Tatterson's? Are you planning on going to their house for Easter? Call soon!

xoxo
Mom & Dad

From: Sissy4short@aol.com
To: Katie356@aol.com

So sad, long time no hear from you! I know you've been busy, me too! About Easter weekend, the party's on! You just *gotta* come!
No pressure there, kiddo!

Sissy

Katie refused to reply to all e-mails and phone calls for another two weeks. Tonie was very alarmed. She was forced to do what she thought was best for Katie. *She called Austin Tatterson.*

She had to leave him a message, saying, "Austin, this is Tonie, remember me, the café owner? Our Katie is in trouble. You said to call if she ever needed anything. Dude, she needs you now! Don't ask me why. I can't tell you. Because as Katie's friend…well, I just can't. If you love her, like I believe we both know you do, you'll come to her *now*. Don't wait! Can you leave today?"

Immediately after listening to his messages, Austin called Katie. Her voice mail picked up his call.

"Katie, call me. This is Austin."

Day one, no return call from Katie.

Day two, no return call from Katie.

Day three, Austin was almost to Katie's apartment when he called her one more time.

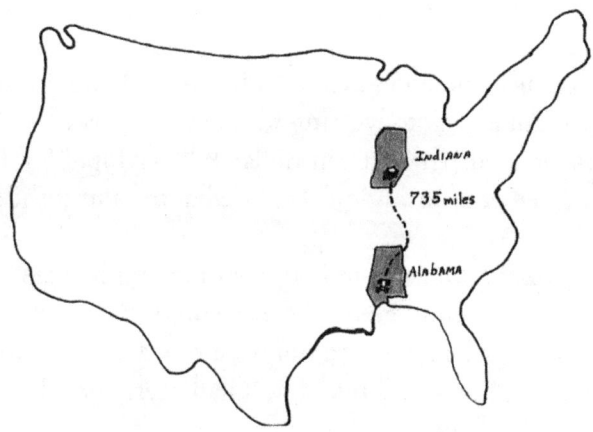

Again, her voice mail picked up.

"This is Austin, remember me? I'm almost in town—Morgantown, that is. I've been trying to get in touch with you for three days now. I'm helping Belinda move out of her apartment. She's moving to California to be closer to her fiancé and his family in Oxnard. Bucky introduced them after we realized that she and I was never going to be a couple. Being a good friend to both, I'll be helping Bucky and Belinda today with the move. We need at least four hours to load the U-Haul, then they'll be on their way. I'll leave from here to go to Colorado for our family's get-together. I'll call when we're done. Maybe we can go grab a bite to eat before I leave. By the way, are you going to my folks'?"

Katie jumped to her feet. She looked around at her apartment.

"What a mess! Think, Katie, think!"

She sprang into action by throwing away all the empty takeout boxes. She made her bed, picked up all the dirty laundry, sprayed Lysol in the air. She hopped in the shower then dressed in real clothes—a pair of jeans and a light-green sweater. Her hair has grown out again, so she pulled it back into a ponytail. Then she put on her favorite pink lip gloss.

Five hours after his phone call, Austin was at Katie's door. *Dingdong, dingdong!* She looked through the peephole. All she could see was a *ten-dollar bill.*

"Austin, is that you?"

"*It's me!*"

Katie opened the door. He had a five o'clock shadow of a beard now and had gone back to wearing his geeky eyeglasses.

Austin handed her that ten-dollar bill, saying, "I was told by Sissy that I owed you this. I don't know what for, but if she says I do, then I do."

Katie took it and began to laugh out loud. "I'll take it, but Sissy will have to tell you why she thinks that you owe it to me!"

That sound of laughter had not been heard in her apartment for quite some time. Come to think of it, it had been since their last visit.

"Katie, I need your help!"

"What can I do, what's wrong?"

Austin explained, "I was pulling off I-33 onto South Main Street, when the *check engine* light came on in my car. I pulled over to the side of the road and called Dad. He called your dad. Your dad said not to drive it, just to get it to a garage and let their mechanic check it out. He said he wishes he could have helped me but the garage really needed to put it on their diagnostic machine to check out my car's computer system. Your dad says he knows very little about these newer cars, anyway. So … I called Smith's Auto Service on Seventh Street. Do you know anything about them?"

Katie shook her head indicating no.

"Oh well, that's where I've been for the last hour. Jim Smith, the owner and lead mechanic there, says that it needs a new alternator and that he'll have to order one. He also says sometimes it takes a week to ten days just to get the part in. Then it will take a half of a day just to put the thing on! I took a taxi to get here. Believe it or not, the driver is the same one that took Sissy and me to the train station. What're the odds? I guess I should play the lottery."

After saying all that, Austin hugged Katie, letting her know that it was sure good seeing her again and that he missed her.

Katie replied, saying, "I missed you too, Austin. But how can I help? I know nothing about cars. Do you need some money? Do you need a place to stay?"

Austin answered, "No, I have money, and even if I did not, I would never take it from you! I just need a lift to Colorado. I was hoping that you took the time off and was planning on going to my parents'. I hear that your parents may be coming.

"Please rescue me…I don't want to take the train! Sissy liked it, but I thought it was just awful! If you agree to take me with you, I'll pay for the gas, the meals, and our stay in the hotel too. *I'll pay for it all.* I did the calculating, and we could easily make it there in two days.

"While waiting on my car's diagnosis, I booked a room here at the Microtel Hotel. Your dad told my dad that it is a good place to stay while I'm here."

Austin walked toward Katie's door, talking hurriedly as he was wanting to get out fast, not giving Katie a chance to refuse before thinking about his request!

"Katie, it would mean the world to me if I could just go with you. *Don't answer now.* Just think about it. Just let me know in the morning. I'll need to leave around ten o'clock. The taxi's still waiting outside, so I need to go now."

Austin leaned in and kissed Katie on her cheek, then he quickly left.

"What a surprise! First his visit and then his kiss."

She hadn't planned on going to Colorado, but how could she tell her friend in need no?

For weeks now, Katie has had her life on hold. Possibly this was exactly what she needed to jump-start it back to life.

"Hey, what about going out for a bite to eat? Oh well, he must have lost his appetite with the bad news about his car! Katie, it's a peanut-butter-and-honey-topped English muffin for you. Again!"

With mixed emotions regarding seeing both her parents and the Tatterson family, Katie reluctantly decided to go. After all, she'll not be able to hide from them forever. She packed for the trip, shaved her legs and armpits, plucked her neglected eyebrows, and was ready to leave the next morning.

Austin left knowing that if he would have asked Katie too far in advance, she might have made up an excuse for not going to Colorado with him. *Whatever it was that Katie was going through*, he was determined to be there for her.

As Austin checked into room 104, he calls Tonie, revealing to her his well-thought-out plan. She thanked him again, begging him not to let her back out of going to Colorado.

"And if she tries to use the café as an excuse, tell her, 'Oh, you know Tonie, she'll cover your shifts. Hasn't she always done that for you?'"

The next morning Katie called Austin around 7:30 a.m. She let him know that she was willing to give him a ride to Denver. (*To himself, Austin quietly gestured "Yes!"*)

"I'll pick you up at ten. I need to get the bug's oil changed and the tires rotated first."

Gentleman Austin said, "I'll pick up the tab for that too."

"No, my grandpa has already sent the money to cover it."

They both agreed that ten o'clock was their rendezvous time.

Katie had to drive past the Women's Clinic to get to Austin's hotel. Many people today accepted abortion as being legal and right. Katie considered herself a law-abiding citizen. She couldn't figure out why then she had all the shame that she was feeling concerning her choice. She had reconciled in her mind not to blame God. She was not even angry with Kurk anymore. For all she knew, he was married by now and had moved on.

Lately, her time in Morgantown had revealed much to Katie. The one revelation that stood out the most was that *she was tired of being alone*! She didn't like it and didn't want it anymore! She quickly returned to her tiny apartment, packing everything else she owned into her car's trunk. She turned in her door key to her landlord, with plans of never looking back.

She picked up Austin a little later than planned. He seemed not to mind. He just loaded his duffel bag onto her back seat, after seeing that her trunk was full.

"Gee, Katie, we're only going for a week. You look like you're moving in."

Katie offered no reply. He then offered to drive, but Katie insisted on staying behind the wheel.

"When did you learn to drive a stick shift anyway?"

"I taught myself in grandpa's old company truck."

"I'm impressed!" Katie said.

Austin took out his directions to Colorado at Katie's request.

"It's almost a straight-shot west, look."

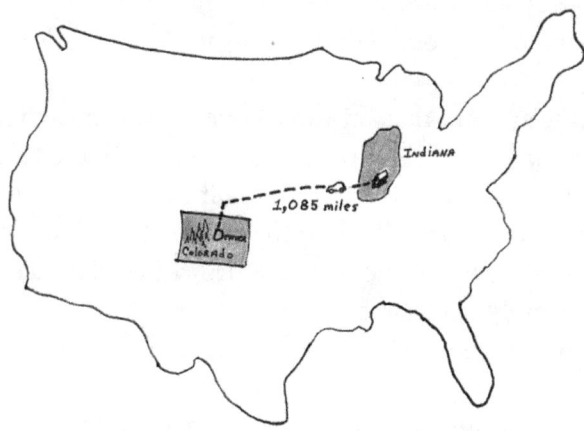

As they journeyed on, it was *not* like old times at all. For this was the first time that they'd ever been alone. They had never even spoken without Sissy's jokes and ramblings on being the center of attention.

(They are two young adults, with only their past memories in common.)

Katie was impressed with what a good man Austin had turned out to be and that he was very knowledgeable about a lot of different topics. She also noticed that he gave her time to talk … allowing her time to express her point of views. He even seemed to care about her dreams and her goals.

That was so refreshing to Katie. He was so thoughtful and attentive…For hours, Katie had forgotten all about Morgantown, Indiana, and everything that it implied.

Katie thought it appropriate to ask how Belinda was doing. He explained all the details concerning her move and that Belinda had said to tell her hi and that if she ever got to Oxnard, California, to look her up. Austin also told her that Belinda recently got some disturbing news.

Nearly paralyzed…Katie thought that perhaps she might have found out about *it* and told Austin. But how could she know?…Did Kurk tell Marsha? Did Marsha tell Belinda?

Oh, I hope not! I don't need any judgments or sympathy from Austin right now!

Reservedly, Katie asked, "What bad news?"

"Remember the couple that got engaged on New Year's Eve?"

"Yes … I do."

"Well, it appears that on their honeymoon in the Caribbean, they went sailing for the afternoon, and neither one of them made it back. The Coast Guard found the sailboat, but they were never found. The Coast Guard called off the search after a few days, saying they both were apparent victims of a drowning. Belinda says both families are simply devastated."

Katie didn't know what to say except, "That's just awful, isn't it?"

Then she abruptly pulled into an approaching rest stop to go to the restroom.

Both shocked and sad, she felt somewhat vindicated that *they got theirs*. Katie normally did not react that way. However, for the first time in weeks, she was able to pray.

"Lord, *forgive me* and forgive them. I pray that they both had time to call upon your name and that they both made it to heaven because they both sure were devilish down here. *Forgive me* for any wrong thinking and my non-Christlike attitude toward them both. And by the way, thank you for making a way for me to get out of Morgantown. *Help me now to leave behind all bitterness and shame.* I need your help in deciding what to do next. I'm at a crossroads here! I don't think I can handle very much more. So we'll have to talk later. Give travel mercies to me and Austin, my parents, Sissy, and her entire family. It's in Jesus's name I pray. *Amen!*"

To mask her red eyes, Katie put on her sunglasses. Austin was walking back to the car from the vending machines, with two cans of soda and a candy bar for each of them.

"Are these okay with you?"

"Sure!"

Quieter than before, Katie was glad to have the candy bar and the cola to sip on to cover her silence.

Back on the road again, Austin pointed at a billboard advertisement.

"Look, a Christmas shop. If you don't mind, let's pull off the next exit. I need to get my mother something. I haven't sent her a gift in a while, and you know how she goes all out for Christmas."

Katie replied, "Sure, sounds like fun."

Santa's year-round gift shop was a neat concept. It was sunny out but with a lot of artificial snow indoors. Austin purchased a figurine of a group of Victorian Christmas caroler's. It even wound up to play "Oh, Holy Night."

"I hope she doesn't already have this one."

Katie went to the counter to purchase Mrs. Tatterson a hostess gift. She chose a basketful of dessert mixes, spices, cookie cutters, and three red-and-green-checked dishtowels. For herself, she bought a gingerbread boy and girl copper cookie cutter.

Austin's phone rang…It was his mother.

"What's up?…I'm with Katie. We're planning on arriving there late tomorrow night."

Katie could hear her happily laughing from where she stood at the store's checkout counter twelve feet away.

She told Austin, "It's too bad that Katie's parents aren't going to be able to make it, but on the bright side, they had a buyer for their house. They said that they needed to stay in Alabama to pay attention to the details of its closing."

"Mom, I'll tell her."

"Also, remember to tell her that they send her their love! See you tomorrow, you two drive safe."

Katie was okay with hearing the news that her parents couldn't make it and that they sold the house. One set of parents at a time was good for her, *especially now under these circumstances.*

They drove another four hours with Austin dozing on and off most of the way. They stopped to eat at Bob's Big Burger, chatting and reminiscing over a basket of cheesy fries. Their hotel was only a mile and a half down the road, so they checked in early.

Austin walked Katie to her room. There he asked for her car keys.

"I'm going to go filler up and check the oil so that first thing in the morning, we can be on our way."

She handed over her keys to Austin.

He laughed when he saw her rabbit's-foot keychain, saying, "I've seen one just like this one. You and my sister must have bought them together, didn't you?"

Katie laughed saying, "How did you guess?"

Searching for the VW's hood release nob, Austin was unable to find it. The 7-Eleven attendant came out to rescue him by showing him that the latch was in the glove compartment.

The young attendant said, "I know where it is, only because my uncle used to have one of these beetle bugs. We used to drive it up on Braxton's vacated airstrip. We sure had a lot of fun in that old thing!"

Austin popped the hood, and in the glove compartment, he noticed three cassette tapes and a Rubik's Cube with only the red side solved.

Returning to the hotel, Austin took that Rubik's Cube in with him. He wanted to see if he could solve it, planning on giving it back to Katie solved, as a surprise—proving once and for all his geekhood.

Morning came, and after eating the hotel's continental breakfast, they were on their way. Being officially halfway to his parents', the sunny day and the fresh air was clean-smelling. So they both decided to ride with all the windows rolled down.

Austin reached into his duffel bag for his sunglasses…pulling out the *solved* Rubik's Cube. He proudly showed Katie his accomplishment. Much to his surprise, she shouted at him!

"Where did you get that?"

"Katie…It was in your glove compartment. I thought you wouldn't mind, so I solved it for you!"

She grabbed it out of his hand and flung it out of her window! (Thank God, there was not a car or a policeman in sight!) Kurk's last attachment to her hit the pavement and shattered into a million pieces!

If Austin would've known his finding the Rubik's Cube and then solving it would have upset Katie to this magnitude, he would never have done it! Katie's reaction troubled him so.

He tried to lighten her mood by saying, "I don't blame you, Katie, I wanted to do that to that *darn cube* a couple of times last night myself."

Katie gave no reply; she just turned on the radio.

Whatever it was that happened to Katie, Tonie was right. She needs me.

Those two weary travelers arrived in Denver at two o'clock in the morning. They entered the Grand Estes Estate Subdivision and found his parents' home without any difficulty. For Austin had called earlier and talked to his mother, and his dad gave him excellent directions. Austin insisted, since it would be in the middle of the night when they would get there, that they not stay up! That they both just needed to go on to bed. His mother, after being prodded by his dad, said okay. She placed a key to the side door under the welcome mat so that they could let themselves in.

Austin's bedroom was at the top of the stairs, and Katie's was right beside of his. Since they both had never been there before, his mother put their names on the door on a Post-it note. Beyond being real tired, they barely made it to their beds. They both agreed that they could have easily slept halfway up the stairs instead.

(The next day, they each commented that they could feel and hear the VW's engine still humming in their heads well into the morning.)

"What the..." Austin awakened to a border collie pup licking him on his face.

His dad said, "Her name is Ginger. We've been thinking that you're never going to wake up, son! It's time to … get up! Your mother and Katie have lunch made for us."

"New house, new dog—Dad, this is cool!"

Katie was humming and cooking with Mrs. Tatterson. She sure liked being in a home again.

"Austin, we should give your mom her gifts, shouldn't we?"

Austin agreed and went to Katie's bug to get them. He also brought in Katie's Bible that had fallen onto the floor of her car.

They gave their gifts proudly. His mother enjoyed receiving their thoughtfulness. And no, she did not *have that one!* Dad said grace. While enjoying their lunch together, Katie passed around the graduation pictures that she kept in her Bible. And they all four shared some laughter as the two told stories of their cross-country adventure. His parents noticed how much those two seemed to enjoy each other's company. (*That was unexpected!*)

Suddenly, as if cold water had been thrown in her face, his mom switched modes by saying, "We only have two days before the get-together begins, so I need help from the both of you. Austin, if you and Katie would take your father's truck and go downtown and do some shopping for me, I would greatly appreciate it. Meanwhile, your father and I will finish getting the house ready. We're expecting about eighteen or so. Also, while you're here, I would appreciate it if you could help your father clean out the garage gutters. I hate seeing him up on that ladder all by himself."

"Sure, Mother, how about tomorrow morning?"

"Sounds good to me, son."

Purchases were all made. Cooking that could be done in advance was completed. All phone calls that came in were handled by Austin's mother. The house was prepared, and the four of them were *pooped!*

Family members started arriving. The first to come was Austin's aunt and uncle with his two cousins. He had not seen them since he was a little boy, mainly because they were the West Coast Tatterson's.

By afternoon, almost everyone had arrived. The men had the barbecue grill smoking. They had been assigned the duty of cooking the proteins while the ladies were buzzing like bees in the kitchen preparing all the side dishes. Katie oversaw desserts. She was up at the crack of dawn preparing two apple pies and one lemon cream pie. She sure was glad to hear that she didn't have to make a cake too. Because Aunt Ree was bringing her Texas sheet cake. (*Just in case you're wondering, yes, she's from Texas.*)

"Guys will be guys!"

Smoke was just rolling from the grill as they threw a Bronco's nerf-football around. The ladies watched from the kitchen window, praying that they would not need the fire extinguisher that Aunt Ree was jokingly holding in her hand.

From the corner of his eye, Austin noticed Katie at the window. He waved, directing her to come out and pass with him.

Since her part of the meal was already prepared, the ladies told her, "Go on out and play ball."

They tossed the football back and forth, as Austin's mother watched from the kitchen window. She thought she saw a little flirting going on.

"Get over here, Austin, and taste these ribs. Do you think they need some sauce on them?"

"Dad, we put plenty of that Kansas City rub on them. They must be delicious! Just spray a little more apple juice on them to keep them tender. I'm going to show Katie mother's garden."

Austin took Katie's hand as they walked toward the property's side garden. They sat on a wooden bench covered with an ivy trellis. Katie could hardly believe what a stunning place his parents lived in. Their home in Clarion was lovely, but this home was *over the top*!

The Tatterson's Colorado home was a Victorian-style house, with white siding and ebony shutters. An English ivy wreath with daffodils and an oversized yellow gingham bow adorned the double entry doorway. It was picture-perfect, with a wraparound porch and white wicker furniture.

Austin's grandpa walked out, escaping to the front porch to finish reading the last chapter of *Moby Dick*.

He let out the puppy by throwing a tennis ball toward Austin, saying, "Here, son, you play with her for a while."

Katie and Austin played with Ginger, hoping to work off some of that puppy energy, as Grandpa had suggested.

"Come and eat, it's ready!"

At the end of the meal, Austin told his parents that he sure did miss their meals together."

Uncle Bobby Long commented, that was the best brisket that he had ever eaten. That was saying a lot since Uncle Bobby was noted for his *barbecuing skills.*

"Mom, before it gets dark, I'm going to take Katie downtown to have a better look around."

"Here, drive my car because in about fifteen minutes, these guys are going to be snoring, and some of us women might be joining them. I know Aunt Ree will."

The kids were in the den playing video games, and Aunt Pauline wanted all the Tatterson women to watch a movie together. She brought *Coal Miners Daughter.* It was a movie about Loretta Lynn's life.

"Sissy Spacek plays Loretta," she said, "and you can't tell them apart." She even sang all the songs in the movie too!

Austin's dad chimed in, saying, "It's best if you two go explore today because the rest of the family gets here tomorrow."

Airports, parks, shops, café's, high rises, American flags, mansions, condos, bungalows, bed and breakfasts, Colorado State flags, schools, sport fields, hospitals, pawn shops, doctor's offices, fitness centers, book stores, vitamin shops, outdoor sports stores, public libraries, specialty food stores, movie theaters, music stores, street musicians, tree-lined boulevards, strip malls, bicycle rentals, spring flowers, a zoo, fresh bakery smells, frozen yogurt shops, stadiums, high-end departments stores, churches, thrift stores, people from all walks of life (the elderly, baby boomers, millennials, and the very young), men walking their dogs and dogs walking men—Denver had it all.

You could say that this city was full of ski culture too! What more could a person ask for? And the *view of the Rocky Mountains!* They took both Katie's and Austin's breaths away.

Grabbing their final cup of coffee for the day, Austin and Katie headed back ... before Mother called out the troops to look for them. Once again, they found his parents' subdivision with no problem. With the streetlights being on now, Katie was blown away at the sight of the Tatterson's Victorian estate. It looked like an actual

Thomas Kincaid portrait. She celebrated and was so happy for them! For they had endured. God blessed them with more than what they would ever ask for or could even think of.

Even though she had to share a bedroom and bathroom with four others, that night she welcomed sleep. The room was overly cluttered, but for the first time in weeks, *Katie's mind was not*. Being surrounded by the Tatterson family…Katie once again felt carefree and lighthearted. She *whispered* her prayers and thanked God for… well…*just for everything*!

The next day was crammed full of family, food, and fun. It was the day before Easter. A lot of prep time was necessary. Tomorrow the group planned on attending sunrise service at the Maranatha Independent Church, where Austin's parents had recently started attending.

Katie set her clock for 4:00 a.m. She thought that she'd have a better chance at that time to have some privacy in the bathroom. She was up and dressed then left the bedroom *quietly* to go downstairs.

Before this morning, she never paid much attention to the portraits and photos that hung on the wall of the Tatterson's stairway. It proudly displayed the Tatterson's family history—photos of parents, grandparents, and great-grandparents: Corey in his military uniform (he was such a handsome guy and so young), one's of Sissy through the years, and Austin too.

How surprised Katie was that many of their memories included her: one with her and Sissy wearing matching Christmas sweaters, one with the Tattersons and her family beach vacationing at Cape Charles in Virginia together, school group photos (some of which she had wished they'd never hang there for all to see).

Katie softly sang "He's Alive" while making a pot of coffee and a pitcher of fresh squeezed orange juice. She also popped in a large batch of her lemon poppy seed muffins into the Tatterson's convection oven. She had never used such a fancy oven…but how hard could it be?

(They came out perfect!)

The Tatterson bunch must have smelled the aroma of the coffee and the muffins baking because they began trickling down the stairs into the kitchen, helping themselves to her delicious yummies!

Sunrise service was simply wonderful! Colorado sunrises were more spectacular than most—pinks, reds, yellows, and oranges. They even had shades of colors that Katie said she had never seen before. What an experience! What a welcomed surprise when Austin reached over and took her hand during the pastor's closing prayer, not letting her go until they got to the car.

Being around Austin these last several days made it possible for Katie to bring herself out of hiding. She was quickly becoming happy again!

"Hey, Katie, I have a joke for you...What type of a bunny can't hop?"

Katie thought for a minute then answered, "I don't know!"

"A chocolate one!" Austin answered, pulling one out of a bag that he had hidden under her passenger seat.

They both shared in a good laugh and in something else too! A much more confident Austin leaned in to kiss Katie. This time it was not planted on her cheek... He kissed her on her tender pink lips. Katie didn't kiss him back. Austin had hoped she would return the affection he had been denied over the years. For her lips were lifeless and as cold as a slab of marble.

Looking at Austin through her new point of view these last several days, Katie had hoped he didn't take her response to his advance wrong. He just startled her; that was all it was!

She paused...and said, "Can we try that again?"

She relaxed into their second kiss. This time she was not kissing Sissy's baby brother. She was kissing Austin, and it came off as being *heavenly.*

Austin became so excited that he blurted out, "Katie, why don't you come back home to Alabama? You can be with me! You can attend the university there!"

Katie placed her hand gently over his mouth. "I can't give you any answer. I never thought I had a reason to go back home."

"Isn't it plain to see that you do *now?*"

Katie replied, "Let me pray about it...okay?"

"That's all the answer I need for now! I think we need to head back to the house because my parents and the whole *Hee-Haw Gang* will be fighting over the best seats at the table. And I may be needed to referee!"

"You're right, I've been at your family's celebrations before. Your dad will more than likely be in the thick of things!"

Katie put her bug into reverse.

Austin quickly said, "Wait, I'm getting hungry, aren't you?"

"Let's eat some chocolate," as Katie took her *joke* out of its bag and bit off the bunny's ears, then handed it over to Austin.

He took his turn by beheading the milk-chocolate bunny.

The entire family was home and gathered together.

Ernie needed to make two announcements. The first one was for the children.

"Kids, we're not going to have an Easter egg hunt. Instead, if you would go all over the house and the yard, hunting for the tennis balls that Ginger has well hidden, I'll give you two dollars for each ball you find and turn in to Grandpa."

(Grandpa was setting in the Barclay lounger with Ginger's empty basket on his lap.)

"The one that finds the most tennis balls gets a crisp new twenty-dollar bill (from grandpa!). Good news for you, there's probably thirty or more of them well hidden! I'll give you one hint…She loves to hide them in shoes, in the bushes, and under pillows. So…get on your mark, get set, and *go*!"

Chaos erupted as they all abruptly scattered.

Turning, Ernie said, "The second announcement is…"

Ernie opened the powder room door, and out jumped Katie's mom and dad. Katie began to cry. She leaped into her daddy's arms, and her mom joined in!

"We thought you weren't coming?"

"Your dad and I wanted it to be a *surprise*!"

"You did it again to me, Mom. Daaaadd, you guys are getting pretty good at this *surprise* thing."

They gave Katie a florescent green beach T-shirt, a large box of saltwater taffy, and a variety of seashells from the Gulf that they had gathered.

"Mom…Dad, look at your tans!"

Katie was amazed to see how quickly they went from pale to copper-toned skins. Next the Vincent's handed the Tatterson's a housewarming gift. It was a hand-crocheted tablecloth, big enough to fit their elegant dining room table for ten. Katie's grandmother made it, taking her all of *eleven months* to complete.

Just then, in popped Sissy through the front door, proclaiming, "And when mother kicks the bucket, I want her to leave that tablecloth to me because Austin doesn't need it. If he'd get it, he'd just ruin it by using it as a napkin!"

The room burst into laughter…and in walked the Reverend Wade Foxx. His arms were full—loaded down with a very large purple-and-black polka-dot suitcase, a small black bag, and a *huge bag* of navel oranges!

Sissy yelled out, "We did it!" showing her family their wedding rings! "Last weekend we went to Florida." Turning to her mother and dad, she said, "Mother…Daddy…*don't be mad!* Dear Reverend James married us there on the beach. That's all the wedding Wade and I really wanted."

Being glad for them, her parents went over to congratulate them both.

"These oranges are from Reverend James. He sends his love to all of you."

Austin gladly shook his new brother-in-law's hand by saying, "Good luck in keeping up with that one! *Thank God*, now it's your turn!"

Austin gave both a *big hug*. When he hugged Sissy, they exchanged whispers.

"What was the ten dollars for?"

"Did you give it to her?"

"Yes, I did, but why…what's it for?"

Still whispering, Sissy replied, "That's for me to know and you to find out!"

Cameras were going off all over the room.

Sissy took Katie over to introduce her to Wade, saying, "Wade, this is my Katie. Katie, this is my Wade." Sissy pulled all three of them in for a group hug.

It was settled…Sissy was the one that was a preacher's wife. That was amazing. What were God and Wade thinking? With her dynamic personality…Willow Creek Baptist Church would never be the same! It was one thing to attend there…it was another to lead! God knows best!

Mr. Vincent spoke out and said, "We also have an announcement to make. We sold our house, it closed on Thursday."

Congratulations came from several folks in the room.

Uncle Troy spoke out, asking, "Do we know the new owners?"

Sissy and Wade spoke with one voice, saying, "We are!" as Wade held up the keys to the front door.

Turning to Katie…Sissy said, "Katie girl, we just had to have it. It already felt like home to me, and Wade loves how close it is to the church. And besides, you remember our growth chart. It's still on your closet door, *we have history there*. No one else would appreciate it like we do. Just think about it, we can continue our tradition by watching our kids *grow up that same door*."

Mrs. Tatterson said, "Now, that's enough announcements for one day, don't you think!"

She then started giving out verbal orders.

"Sissy, you put the new tablecloth on the dining room table. Katie, you and your mom can set the tables. You men," directing with her hands, "can get the card tables and set them up there," pointing to an open space in front of the living rooms and the dining rooms huge bay windows.

"There're two tables in the kitchen pantry. The rest of you can go down to the basement and bring up the extra folding chairs. The ham and the pot roast is ready. All I have to do is a couple little things in the kitchen, and then we'll be ready to say grace."

"Mom, the table is set." Sissy turned her attention to her family that had gathered in the kitchen, saying, "Wade really needs to lighten up a little. He refuses to call my deviled eggs, deviled eggs. He prefers that I call them stuffed eggs."

The ladies began to laugh, but her grandmother squelched it quickly by saying, "Ladies, I see nothing wrong with that. From now on," holding up her tray of deviled eggs, "I rename these stuffed eggs!"

"Yes, ma'am," Sissy said.

Also the entire room full of Tatterson cooks unanimously agreed with Grandmother's renaming! After all, Grandmother *ruled* the kitchen.

Ernie deferred the blessing to his new son-in-law, Reverend Wade. He did an eloquent job. Then the famished group dug in. Food was on each table—hands moving, mouths chewing, and utensils clanging. It was the best way to spend a holiday together. (*Don't you agree?*)

Leftovers were put away, and the dishes were done. Everyone found a comfortable place to relax, both indoors and out—each one finding a family member or friend to talk to. Sissy and Wade, at her parents' suggestion, retreated to the downstairs bedroom for a nap.

Katie and her dad walked out to the driveway to look at the Super Beetle.

"How's she doing, honey?"

"She's just fine, Dad. I check and change the oil and rotate the tires just like you told me to!"

He could not help but notice the packed boxes in the trunk. "Gee, little girl, why all the boxes?"

She quickly made up an excuse as her mom yelled for the two of them to meet her in the sunroom.

There were Austin's parents, her mom, and now the two of them. Those five shared a cup of coffee as they talked over the future.

Katie's mom started the conversation, saying, "We were standing on the balcony of the condo when we decided that the Gulf of Mexico is beautiful and all as a vacation destination goes, but beach life is *not* for us."

Don said, "All we know at this point is that we want a small home to enjoy and to live in for the rest of our lives. More importantly, we want to get our lives out of storage!"

"Well, Don," Ernie said, "have you considered moving to Colorado? Are you looking for a part-time job? If so, my plant really needs a good diesel mechanic. You'd only have to work two or three days a week. Condos around here are the only way to go for semi-retirees. If you should decide to move here, you'll definitely need to learn how to ski. And just as we've had to, you'll get real good at planning your winter weekends around the snow reports."

Don replied, "Skiing has to be a whole lot better than deep-sea fishing."

Katie excused herself, allowing the four of them time to make their plans.

Austin was in the family room, playing cards with his grandpa. The kids were busy counting their tennis ball money. Ginger was circling the basket that now held twenty-four tennis balls.

Grandpa said, "*Thank God*, that should keep her busy for the rest of the day!"

Katie took advantage of the crowd's busyness to disappear for some quiet time. She walked outside onto the backyard, going for the serenity of the flower garden. Katie found Denver's late-afternoon air clean and riveting. She prayed, thanking God for Sissy and Wade being able to purchase her childhood home and for her mom and dad's surprise visit, also for the likelihood of her parents' moving to Colorado.

And most of all, for Austin's kiss! She could hardly get her mind off it. She believed that Austin was in love with her.

Could he be God's best for me? Is it remotely possible that I am falling in love with him too?

"Rummy, I win!"

Austin left the game to go and find Katie. When the two met, they embraced and kissed. Holding hands, they decided to walk through the neighborhood. After watching another Colorado sunset in Washington Park, they headed back to the party.

Along the way, Austin asked, "Tell me, Katie, why the 3-5-6 in your e-mail address?"

She explained that it was Reverend James's favorite scripture: Proverbs 3 verses 5 and 6.

"Do you know what it says?"

Austin answered, "Of course I do! It says, '*Trust in the Lord with all your heart, lean not to your own understanding, acknowledge him in all your ways, and he will direct your path.*'"

"That's right! Reverend James explained those Bible verses to me this way. Verses 5 and 6 cover the *three* most important things that we are to do regarding every circumstance in our life, especially in our relationship with God. By doing these *three* things, it then obligates the Lord to direct our paths through this life. He said that we must *trust in the Lord* with all my heart, by *never trying to figure out* the who, what, when, where, and the how's *with our own intellectual understanding*. Then as we acknowledge him in everything, good or bad, in all things, not just some things, but in all things, the *Lord then becomes obligated to give us the directions* we so desperately need throughout our entire life. After his explanation, they too have become my favorite scriptures. So naturally, I wanted to include my favorite scriptures in my e-mail address. It's much better than SmartfartKT that Sissy suggested!"

"Do you know that you're the only person that has ever asked me that question? I'm impressed."

"Katie, by now, the family must be wondering where we disappeared to."

They went inside, but not before Austin got another kiss from Katie.

"Katie, are you ever going to say you'll marry me?"

"Why, Austin Tatterson, *you have never asked me to marry you!*"

"I've asked you to marry me several times, thank you!"

"No...you have never asked me. *You've always told me* that you were going to marry me!"

After that comment, Katie ran inside.

Austin remained outdoors, thinking, "You know, she's right! I've never asked her to marry me. Well, I'm going to have to remedy that!"

He ran upstairs, searching for his mother. He found her restocking the bathrooms with clean towels.

"Mother, do you have a minute?"

"Sure, come into my bedroom and sit down. What's on your mind, son?"

"Remember great-grandmother Tatterson's emerald ring?"

"Yes!"

"You once told me that it was mine when I found the girl that I wanted to propose to."

"Yes, I remember."

"Can I have her ring now?"

With tears in her eyes, she answered, "You sure can, it's always been yours like I'd promised."

She walked over to her jewelry box and handed him the ring, saying, "You know, son, it's a beautiful engagement ring, isn't it? Especially for a young lady whose *favorite color is green*."

The family had left, traveling their different routes in going home. The Tatterson's Victorian calmed down once again. Instead of going sightseeing as suggested by Sissy, the group opted on staying in and making ham and pot roast sandwiches and watching a movie. Sissy and Wade, Austin and his parents, and Katie and her parents took their sandwiches into the Tatterson's family room and comfortably sat to watch Ernie's DVD choice of Mel Gibson's *The Passion of Christ*.

Austin appeared unusually nervous. He stood to announce, "Wait a minute, before we start, I too have something to say!"

Sissy spoke up and says, "Another announcement, enough already! What have you done now, little brother?...Dad just put the movie in!"

Her mother spoke up and said, "*No!* Let him talk...It's Austin's turn!"

"Sissy, it's not what I did. It's what I'm about to do! Katie Vincent, this is not a sudden thing, and it should be of no surprise to anyone in this room, especially since I have been telling you all my life that I was going to marry you. Just recently it has been brought to my attention—by someone who means the world to me—that I've never asked you to marry me. Katie Vincent, that's what I'm doing now."

Austin got down on one knee and showed her his great-grandmother's emerald ring.

"I'm not sure if anyone still does it like this, but here goes. If it's all right with you, Mr. and Mrs. Vincent, I want Katie to become my bride."

With Don Vincent's giving his nod of approval, Austin was free to continue.

Katie took the ring and considered his blue eyes and said, "It's true, you've been wanting to marry me as far back as I can remember. But tell me one thing, do you love me?"

"Yes, I love you. I've always loved you, Katie."

She responded by saying, "I can now say that I love you too. Yes, Austin Lane Tatterson, *I will marry you.*"

He slipped on the slightly oversized emerald heirloom ring onto her ring finger and sealed his proposal with a passionate kiss.

After their embrace, they turned to scan the room for their families' reactions. All they saw were three couples kissing and hugging each other.

Austin looked at Katie and said, "I believe they all approve!"

Katie's mom gleefully said, "We have a lot of planning to do!" While the men just looked at each other and started eating their sandwiches, *with grins* on their faces.

"Mom, let's not get in any hurry. Austin and I have some talking to do first, then we'll begin to plan."

Ernie said, "But for now, we'll watch my movie, right? Then we can get some sleep!"

With that announcement, the three men give out a big sigh of relief, as Ernie popped in his movie.

Sissy chimed in, "What just happened here? Is anybody else as surprised as I am?"

Sitting beside her parents on the Tattersons' butter-soft leather sofa, Austin held Katie secure in his arms.

Sissy had a hard time keeping her concentration on the movie as she kept staring over at Katie and Austin, thinking, *My little brother, my best friend getting married? I didn't even know they were dating. I can hardly believe what I am seeing and hearing. Super? Super!*

"Mom, isn't that Great-Grandmother's ring? Katie, just for your information…you might want to get it professionally cleaned. I wore it playing dress up when mother wasn't looking, and I accidently dropped it in the toilet bowl. I had to fish it out by using my Rainbow Bright fishing pole. You're lucky…I only had to do a number 1 and not a number 2! Good night, folks!" Sissy grabbed Wade's hand and whisked him away to their downstairs love nest!

"Now, Katie and Austin, don't you think for one moment that I didn't notice a soggy wad of toilet paper with a ring inside on my dressing table. I took the ring to Feaster's Jewelers and had it professionally cleaned the next morning after dropping you both off at preschool. And since it's *come-clean* time...Katie, I knew that Tiger didn't break my bottle of perfume now, did she?"

"No, ma'am. But how did you know?"

"First, we need to work out that *ma'am* title since we're going to be family now, aren't we?"

"Yes, ma'am—I mean, yes, Mrs. Tatterson..."

"Michelle, please...you can call me Michelle. To answer your question. First, I know my daughter, and if Tiger would have broken my perfume bottle, she would have smelled like Chanel number 5. Instead she just smelled like her Hartz flea collar. And Austin, Sissy didn't put that dent in my new car now, did she?"

The next morning, both mothers got up early to make their family a good breakfast—consisting of French toast, bacon, fresh strawberries, and French-pressed coffee. Over breakfast, the parents had a chance to process both Sissy and Wade's marriage and Katie and Austin's engagement while those four slept in.

The Vincent's and Tatterson's had always acted like family, but now with an approaching wedding, they officially would soon be... one BIG *happy family.*

Katie and Sissy, Wade and Austin finally made their way to the coffeepot. Dad pulled out his trusty Polaroid camera. It was identical to the one he bought Sissy for her sixth birthday. The group could hardly believe their eyes. That old thing still worked? They were more surprised that he could still get film and flashbulbs for it.

Ernie said, "I can still get the film through the Polaroid factory and flashbulbs through some collectors, but they're getting harder to come by."

"Come on, you two," he said, speaking to Sissy and Wade, "while your mother's making your French toast, let me take your picture. After all, we need a wedding picture for the family wall! Katie and Austin, you're next. Now show me that ring. Say cheeeese!"

The flash went off. Katie asked for her a copy too. So the flash went off again.

Austin whispered into Katie's ear, "We'll leave around eleven, if that's okay with you?"

She nodded, "Yes."

They enjoyed another hour of conversation around their delicious breakfast meal.

When Austin's mother asked, "What time, Katie, are you planning on leaving?"

"Around eleven."

"And you, Austin?"

"Mother, remember, I'm going back with Katie to get my car?"

"Oh, that's right! I forgot!"

Sissy chimed in, saying, "What about Austin's car? It's still parked in the church's parking lot, isn't it?"

Austin shot Sissy a hate-stare.

She sheepishly replied, "Oops! Did I say something wrong?"

Katie looked at Austin. "You didn't really break down, did you?"

"*No*, I rented a car to come to your place."

"You lied to me? Did you even help Belinda move?"

"*No*, she moved a month ago. But she did say if you're ever in California, for you to look her up."

"So let me get this straight, you lied about your car and you lied about helping Belinda move too?"

A shaken Katie ran outside upset. Her mom and Sissy followed her. Austin got up to run after her too, but both Don and Ernie looked at each other and stopped Austin from leaving.

Ernie stepped in front of the patio door, saying, "Sit down, son. Finish your coffee."

Don said, "This is going to take awhile, but trust me in saying this, it's going to be all right! Just let the women handle this one."

After both her mom and Sissy reasoned with her, explaining that Austin's motives were good ones, Katie's mom asked her the one important question that she demanded Katie to answer.

"If he wouldn't have shown up in Morgantown, would you still have come to Colorado?"

Katie answered, "Probably not, Mom."

"Then you would have been a fool to have missed out on this family get-together, not to mention your very own engagement to *one of the nicest men on planet Earth*."

Katie agreed! Now feeling horrible for calling Austin out in front of his family, she ran toward the house.

Austin met her in the yard, and they both take turns saying their apologies, followed by some heavy embracing.

Sissy walked by and yelled, "Get a room, you two."

Katie's mom, walking behind Sissy, said, "You better not—not until your wedding night, you don't!"

Katie had forgotten about the wedding night.

As Austin began packing the VW, his dad and his soon-to-be father-in-law were ribbing him by saying, "Didn't we tell you that they'd work it out *for you*? When you've been married as long as we have, you'll understand women better! Until then…we'll just have to help you get through it!"

Katie took a moment with her mom and dad to say their goodbyes…when down the stairs came flying Sissy and Wade with both of his arms full to the max. He was wearing his tacky Florida groom T-shirt, and Sissy was wearing her tacky Florida bride T-shirt.

As usual, she interrupted—this time by jumping into Katie's arms, saying, "You're not going to make me wear one of those god-awful poufy bridesmaid's dresses, are ya?"

Katie sassed back, "No, you're going to wear a god-awful puffy matron of honor dress. Ha-ha-ha!"

Austin's mom and dad joined in and sent Sissy and Wade on their merry way.

Next to leave were Katie's mom and dad.

Then Katie asked Michelle for an envelope, a sheet of paper, and a pen. She asked Ernie if he could mail a letter out for her.

He said, "Sure, I can mail it out tomorrow, and there's no need for you to buy postage, I have a roll of stamps right here."

Dear Tonie,

Look at my Polaroid picture first. You were 100% right. It happened when I least expected it. It's a long story and not enough ink to tell it. Austin and I are engaged! I'm moving back to Alabama. I'll be attending the university there. Regretfully, I must resign my position at the Gingerbread Café. Thanks for everything! And I mean, everything!

Love, your friend,
Katie Vincent, soon-to-be
Mrs. Austin Tatterson!

P.S. Hope you, Neil, and Jo Ann can make it to our wedding. I'll send you guys an invite.

(To this day, if you stop by the Gingerbread Café, at the corner of Highland and Center Avenues, in Morgantown, Indiana, you'll see that same framed Polaroid picture of Katie and Austin hanging on the back wall.)

Chapter Eight

Meanwhile, Back in Madison!

LAST FALL WAS A SHORT season for the citizens of Madison, Arkansas, as winter weather arrived early with a forecasted *Nor-Easter*. Its heavier snowfall totals, were more than what was predicted. It even caught both channel 13 meteorologist Sam Dunn and farmer Ben Rogers by surprise. In fact, this was the first snowy Thanksgiving that Ben and Sally could ever remember having on Bethesda Acres Farm!

With that snow's abrupt arrival, Ben had no other choice but to stop working his land. Now, he could only wait until the ground thaws in the spring to resume those chores. Winter was calm and picturesque, and it was certainly welcomed at the Rogers household, more than you might suppose.

Ben kept busy sketching, planning, and relaxing in front of the television set, spending hours in his easy chair beside a warm glowing fire. He watched football games and NASCAR races. His favorite driver was Tony Stewart—nickname *Smoke!*—Not forgetting to mention His weekly obligation of shelling Sally's pecans.

For Sally's Thanksgiving cakes, he shelled fifteen cups of nuts. For Christmas, he shelled twenty-four cups. Today during breakfast, Sally informed him that he needed to shell fourteen cups for her Easter cakes. That was just fine with him, since Easter was right around the corner.

After the breakfast dishes were washed, dried, and put away, Sally asked Ben if she could look at his sketchpad.

She commented, "I think this is your best sketch so far of Little Lester (his miniature horse) and Champ (his beagle dog) at the meadows gate."

After seeing that sketch, it gave Sally an idea for Ben's birthday present. She took that sketch to Manley Signs in neighboring Verona, asking Paul to make Ben a new farm entrance sign, one to replace that faded old one her parents had hand-painted so many years ago.

"Paul, I want Ben's horse and dog sketch to be in the center of the sign. Can you do that for me?"

… As for Sally, fall ended the day that she completed the counting of the remaining dried cornstalks in Ben's front cornfield. Then taking Ben's sickle, she cut down the fifty-six stalks that were leftover.

"Three thousand five hundred and sixty-two being the number of abortions performed daily here in America."

Just as Sally reached the last stalk that needed to be removed, the snow began to fall. She was kind of glad because the front cornfield was next on Ben's cleanup list. For he had hopes in plowing *her* field under to plant a cover crop. Sally *was not* yet ready, to let go of her field project!

Ever since that Sunday when Pastor Palmer gave his congregation those abortion statistics, Sally felt a *deep burden to pray for mothers everywhere and for the 3,562!*

Sally had never been an activist. She viewed herself just a childless wife that loved God, loved her country, and cared for people of all ages. As often as she could, Sally bundled up by layering her clothes and walked out to the front cornfield to pray. Passersby and neighbors might only see Ben's neglected front cornfield, but Sally saw it as God's handiwork—because each stalk represented little lives that were once connected to their mothers.

Out in that same cornfield, Sally would often walk, talking to God, questioning him, "Why me? … Why am I so heavily laden with those statistics? Why am I am so moved to pray for mothers?"

Weeks of praying and sketching took place in the Rogers household. Finally, Valentine's Day arrived. Ben and Sally's church was giving a couple's banquet in the church's fellowship hall. Pastor and Mrs. Palmer sat down on Ben and Sally's right side, and the Joneses sat on their left. Ben spoke extensively to Jim and Marcy Jones.

Reverend Palmer seized the opportunity to ask Sally, "Why do you seem troubled as of late?"

"You're right Pastor, I have been troubled." Sally went on to tell him about those *3,562 cornstalks* left standing in Ben's front field and how to her *they represented the babies that were aborted in America each day.*

Reverend Palmer told her that he knew the number all too well.

She went on to ask him, "Why do you think that God chose me to carry such a burden? Why does it mean so much to me? Why, I've never had an abortion! I don't even know anyone who has!"

He spoke out, "You mean, *you think* you don't know anyone that has had one!"

I wonder, does he know something that I don't know? Sally thought.

He went on to say, "Not all women who abort their babies come from dysfunctional families or live in large cities. Most of them just find themselves in *toxic relationships* and can see no other way out. Believe it or not, Sally, some women who abort their babies have even been *raised in Christian homes*. But due to a thinking error, they justify their choice in having an abortion. Often they *cloak their shame with silence* to avoid any stigma of being labeled a *baby killer*.

"Sally, I believe God's answer as to why he has chosen you is *a simple one*. Knowing you the way I've gotten to know you, *you're exactly the one that he would choose*. As a rule, you don't judge others. Even your love for people includes the doctor that aborts, the mothers that abort, and the nurses that assist. Most of all, *you care for these babies that have been aborted*. Why, even out of your own mouth I heard you say 'that you pray each day for the aborted baby's fathers, that your heart goes out to them, as well!' I have never met anyone that has ever considered those fathers as an *important part* of the equation like you do."

"But me!"

The best answer that Reverend Palmer gave her was, "*Child, you're more than what you think you are!* Why don't you spend some time in prayer this week, talking with the Lord. Focus on asking him what's next for you and your *ministry*."

Just hearing the word *ministry* gave Sally the chill bumps. She had never considered herself as one to ever have a ministry.

"Is that what this is? *Oh my!*"

Ben turned to Sally, asking her, "Pass the salt and pepper, please."

The church's youth group began serving their baked chicken and roasted vegetable celebratory meal.

The following day, Sally began her morning as usual, *in prayer*. She then cleaned a little, washed a load of laundry, and did some light cooking. Sally had been a farm girl all her life, and that had sharpened her skills in time management. (She got a lot done in a little amount of time.)

That afternoon, she took advantage of the pleasant weather to clean her front windows, both inside and out. With every spray of the Windex and every swipe of her cotton cloth, *Sally replayed the conversation she had with Reverend Palmer*. Just as she was preparing to clean her last window when she noticed that their baby's white crosses were lying on the ground.

The weight of the snow accumulation must have knocked them over, since this winter Madison got twenty-three inches of the white stuff. Sally stopped her cleaning and walked over to her mother's corner flower bed to set them upright again. Usually, she would tend to her flower garden then be on her way, but not today!

Much later, the only way Sally could explain what happened next... was that an angel was sent from heaven to bring her a special message.

God's angel was all white with large wings that had a wingspan that covered Ben's front cornfield. He *spoke* to her, saying only four *harmonious* words: *"But what about these?"*

Instantly Sally knew what was expected of her. She and Ben had made a memorial for their three babies. Now they too must make a memorial for these *3,562 little ones.*

"They too must be remembered, *that's what he wanted!*" Sally felt chastened but not in a condemning way. She now realized that during the last several months, God had been opening her heart to include them. "Now he must think I'm ready, that I'm up for the challenge to make this memorial space happen!"

Sally looked at those tattered cornstalks and saw a *vision* of what God intended the memorial to look like. He wanted each cornstalk to be replaced with a tiny white cross. The image of Ben's cornfield of crosses took her breath away...as the angel left.

His instructions rendered Sally speechless. She ran into her kitchen. It's amazing how time spent with a little flour, eggs, oil, sugar, and coco would give a lady time enough to do some heavy thinking.

It was two thirty in the afternoon, and Little Lester and Champ alerted Sally that Ben was back from Verona. He went there to pick up some feed and to do an errand for Sally. She sent Ben to Manley Signs for a parcel pickup since Manley's didn't deliver that far out in the county. Paul gave Ben strict instructions *not to open* the tightly sealed container. *Sally wanted it as it was!*

Ben walked through his front door. Sally greeted him with a loud "*Happy birthday!*"

She presented him with a triple-layered chocolate cake, topped with milk chocolate frosting.

Ben handed her Manley's container, but she ricocheted it right back at him.

"What?" he said.

"Ben, you picked up your very own birthday present!"

With no hesitation, Ben tore into it, revealing that it was a new farm sign that she had specially ordered just for him! He was in tears.

"Well, Ben Rogers, I've only seen you cry less than a handful of times in my life, you big baby, you!"

He answered, "I can't help it. I think some sawdust from Manley's shop must have gotten into my eyes when I opened the parcel."

The real reason why he choked up so was the fact that his wife thought enough about his sketch of Little Lester and Champ that she took it and had a sign made with his two furry friends as the farm's *main subjects.*

Sally cut his cake and poured the birthday boy a tall glass of milk to wash it down. After eating not one, but two pieces, Ben went on his way to replace that old sign with his new one, but not before Sally had a chance to share with him what was now on her heart.

Sally told Ben of the burden she had been carrying and of her recent prayer focus. She went on to describe today's visit from the angel that God had sent. Sally needed Ben's blessing in her ministry; after all, it was his front cornfield. She knew part of their livelihood would have to be abandoned to do God's will in this matter.

Ben said, "So that I understand you correctly, you want to put a tiny white cross, like the ones I made for our three babies, beside each cornstalk, then remove the stalks and leave the crosses—*3,562 of them*? Honey, that would mean I'll not be able to plant the front field, meaning smaller profits for us."

"I know, Ben, but my cake sales are up, and I am thinking about talking with Carol to see if she wants to add a few pies to my order each week. By doing this, that will surely make up the difference. As for the crosses, I have enough money saved in my emergency tin to pay for the materials to make them."

Sally poured out on the kitchen table the total sum of $255.10.

"I don't know exactly *why me*. I don't know why God chose here on old Route 707 in Madison, Arkansas. One thing I do know is that we need to take this *giant step of faith* to please our Heavenly Father and that he is asking us to make a difference in a lot of lives. Honey, you don't have to say yes or no right now. Just pray about it, and we'll talk in a few days."

"*That's fair, I'll do just that.*"

Ben walked out the back door, going down the drive to hang his birthday gift. He appeared not to be in any great hurry. At one point, Sally noticed that he looked a little distracted. She watched him while sweeping the front porch and shaking the dirt off the "*Welcome*" mat.

Ben motioned for Sally to come and see the new sign after it was mounted. It was just what she wanted for her Ben. It was fitting that Little Lester and Champ should have their place on the Rogers new farm sign.

Other homeowners posted their Neighborhood Watch signs and ADT Security signs in their front yards. Well, the Rogers are fortunate enough to have animated ones!

Ben turned his attention from Sally's gift toward her soft face, saying, "Sally, I need you to call Paul Manley tomorrow."

"Why, is there something wrong with the sign?"

"No, there's nothing wrong with the sign, I need you to place an order for another sign."

"What sign?"

"One with those abortion statistics on it and we need to post them right there," pointing to the cornfield facing the edge of the road.

"I saw him too! I saw your angel! He told me that God requires this field for his kingdom's purpose and that I am supposed to put an *abortion statistics sign* right there, next to your *3,562 white crosses*!

"The sign that I was shown had those statistics Reverend Palmer gave us months ago in our Sunday bulletin. Do you just happen to have yours?"

Sally said, "*I do!* I use my copy as my Bible bookmark."

"Also, we need to call Reverend Palmer to see if he can come out one day next week, don't we?"

"Yes, I believe we do. This week I'll buy the supplies and make the crosses so we can get them in their rightful places."

Ben was busy that entire week making those *3,562 crosses*. He painted each one white. He numbered each one to ensure that he built the right amount. After they dried, he cut a cornstalk to the ground and replaced it with a tiny white cross.

"*What a sight to behold!*" Paul Manley said.

"Paul, what a surprise seeing you here! I was coming by this afternoon to pick up the sign. This morning Sally said that you had left a message telling us that the sign was done and was ready for pickup."

Paul answered, "Truthfully…I just had to see for myself what all the fuss was about. *You two sure have everyone talking*. I just came from Tommy's Barber Shop, and all the guys were laughing, saying that Madison has its own *Field of Dreams*! I didn't think too much of their jesting. Here, let's get this sign off my truck, and I'll help you to *get'er* in the ground."

A few passersby and even Carol stopped by to ask Ben what in the world he was up to.

He told Carol as well as the others exactly what they were doing. Most of them just shook their heads and drove away. *But not Carol.*

Carol, usually would have said a few choice words that Ben and Sally must ignore to remain her friend. However, today that was not the case. *No back talk, no cursing* at all! Ben was very surprised because out of everyone, he expected opposition and ridicule from her the most. Much to his surprise, her nod and facial expression was that she agreed with their project.

Reverend Palmer dropped by as requested. He had driven by earlier that week to witness Sally and Ben's labor of love. After that, he drove by *every day*, checking on their progress.

Today he got out of his car and joined Sally and Ben in their field.

Addressing Sally, he said, "Often it's something someone says or does that enables a person to believe in themselves. They then find the courage to do what some *may* call controversial. I've been praying about your ministry here. This is a good thing you've done! I believe now you should *start a journal*. You need to tell their stories as they are told to you. Sally thought, "What stories?" "Who knows, God may even ask you Sally, to *write a book.*"

"Wouldn't that be something," Ben said, "an author in the family!"

Mrs. Palmer pulled up the Rogers drive to join her husband already in the field with Ben and Sally. She presented Sally with a beautiful paisley print journal. Embossed in gold was a quote by J. J. H: *"Wisdom cries out that you do not have to experience something to understand it!"* The four of them joined hands to pray over the field of tiny white crosses.

Reverend Palmer left, saying, "This is just a small part of a larger picture. Go one day at a time, and God will direct your path. Their stories," pointing to the crosses, "will bring a lot of meaning to your vision here."

Easter morning arrived. Ben and Sally were busy getting ready for sunrise service when they heard a knock at the front door.

"Who could that be, it's five o'clock in the morning?" Ben said as he hurried downstairs.

"Ben, who is it?"

Ben yelled back to Sally, "It's only Carol!"

He opened the door, and Carol repeated mockingly, "It's only *Caarool!*"

Ben said, "You know what I mean," as he gave her an early-morning hug.

"Well, never mind with all that. I came over because I need a favor from Sally."

Sally was almost to the door, asking, "What favor can I do for you, just *Caarool?*"

Carol lightly tapped her on the shoulder and said with half of a smile. "It looks like the restaurant will sell out of cake by midday tomorrow. This will leave my customers without any desserts. I know it's short notice, but can you bake four pies by tomorrow morning, *please, please, pretty please?* If you'll do this for me, when you deliver them, I'll give you *twelve dollars* a pie and *fill up your gas tank* as a bonus. Why pies? The strangest thing happened…All weekend long, we had several requests for homemade pies."

Ben and Sally happily put their heads together then gave Carol a reply. "Sure, that sounds doable. We were thinking just yesterday about talking to you to see if you would like for me to begin adding a few pies to my weekly order?"

"We'll see how they sell tomorrow, then we'll talk."

Sally replied, "Fair enough! I'll bake two lemon pies, one chocolate, and one coconut cream."

Ben added, "All with mile-high meringue on top, of course."

"That settles it then, see you tomorrow!" Then Carol rushed out with her flashlight on.

"Hey, Carol, happy Easter!" Ben said.

Usually Carol would come back, mocking his faith, *but not today*! Today she simply replied, "And a happy Easter to the both of you too! Oh, another thing, Sally, can you bake one more pound cake, just in case?"

"Well, that settles it!" Ben said. "I know now there's a God. What's up with her? I was just getting used to her nonsense. Now I'm going to have to adjust my feelings toward her."

Sally said, "Come on, Ben, let's grab a mug of coffee and get going. If we don't, we're going to be late! *The sun is about to rise!*"

The next morning, Sally was up at 4:00 a.m. She put her signature southern pecan pound cake in the oven. She collected more eggs from the henhouse to fill Carol's pie order. She shaved the dark chocolate, toasted the fresh coconut, and squeezed eight lemons—*all before 6:00 a.m.* Then she must stop to make Ben his ham-and-egg breakfast that she had promised him.

Carol's extra cake was baked, cooled, dusted, wrapped, and *ready to go*. Four pies cooled on their counter racks.

"Carol has already called twice. I better get these over to her before she has a kitten!" laughed Sally.

"Sally, wait! I'll help you, let's take my truck. This time the gas is on just *Caarool*," chuckled Ben.

After carefully packing Sally's desserts into his pickup, they drove across the road to Carol's Place. Ben pulled up to pump number 1 to get his free fill-up *first*. Sally noticed a vintage-green Volkswagen at the pump next to them. It belonged to a young couple. Their license plate told Sally that they were from Indiana. Ben got his freebie then pulled forward to unload the cake and pies. Of course, Carol was waiting impatiently at the door.

Austin was filling up Katie's bug when she got out to read the sign that was posted across the road (the one in Ben and Sally's front field). With Austin to her back, Katie began to tear up. Sally could not take her eyes off Katie as she stood there looking toward their field of crosses.

Austin called out to Katie, letting her know that the bug was full and that the oil level was fine. He said that he was going to pull forward and park so they could get a bite to eat there at the diner.

Without turning to look at Austin, Katie replied, "Go on in, I'll join you in a few minutes."

Then she walked over to the covered picnic pavilion that Carol had added to her roadside empire summer before last.

At that point Ben noticed Sally's attention being on Katie. Then they *both* noticed the young lady wiping away some tears. Sally looked over at Ben with that look that he had seen over the years. It was the look that said, "I'm on a mission…Someone's in need of my attention more than you do at this moment."

Ben said, "Just go on, I'll go on in and have Carol cut me a piece of that chocolate pie and pour me a cup of her watered-down coffee."

Ben proudly turned and walked through Carol's door just a-*smilin'*. For he just loved hearing his old cowbell that he installed on the diner's door, especially since it was announcing him as Carol's next hungry customer.

Sally walked over and took a seat on a bench close to where Katie was standing. Ben noticed that the only customer that he didn't recognize was sitting at the bar. So he had to be the VW's owner. He sat beside Austin and introduced himself. Ben, knowing his Sally all too well, knew that this might take awhile, so he thought he'd better keep this young man company.

"Carol, I'll have a cup of coffee. And for you, young man?"

"I'll have a glass of water with lemon please, and can I look at a menu? I'll wait for my fiancée before I place our order."

Ben spoke up and said, "Carol doesn't have menus. What she serves is written on the wall."

Ben held silent his next comment, thinking it instead, *You must not know a lot about women, son! Chances are you're going to be here awhile!*

Sally offered Katie a tissue as she introduced herself. She broke the ice by telling her what tears really were.

"Tears are liquid prayers—prayers that only a heart can offer. God designed them so that only he alone understands the reason why they are being shed."

Katie then cried out loud.

Sally went over to hold her, saying, "Honey, you go ahead and cry, get them all out! *It's okay*!"

Those two little words brought such healing to Katie's heart. Later, the only way she could explain what "*It's okay*" felt like was that they made her heart feel like it was dipped in warm honey.

At that point, Austin was at the diner's door to see what was taking Katie so long.

Ben told young Austin, "Your water's here!"

Returning to the bar, Austin told Ben, "I just don't understand it. Coming down the road, Katie was laughing and complaining how hungry she was. Now she's outside crying!"

"I know, but trust me, Austin, she's in good hands! The lady she's with is my wife. So … why don't you and I get a bite to eat and we'll chat for a while."

Carol took the opportunity to ask Ben if he would replace a light bulb in her storage room.

"For Pete's sake, Carol, I'll have to go get my ladder! I can help you out after the Astro-Pirates game. But for now, just bring us a couple of cheeseburger deluxe, an extra-large order of onion rings, and two chocolate shakes! *You have two hungry men sitting here*! Austin, does that order sound good to you?"

"Yes, sir, sounds real good to me."

Ben started their dinner conversation by letting Austin know that he'd been married to Sally for a long time.

"And after all these years, I still haven't been able to figure out her moods and what triggers them. So I don't know if I'm the man to give you any advice. All I can do is give you a bunch of words and hope for the best results."

"Sir, I would feel better if I knew what happened. One thing I do know is that something has happened to Katie and not just today. I think it started a few months ago."

"Son, life is complex, and we *men* just want to get on with it. *Women*, on the other hand, like to take their time to dissect and savor each moment."

"Thank you, Carol. Everything looks good *as always*. Can we have another container of dipping sauce for the onion rings?" Ben, holding up an onion ring, said, "Like this onion ring … how do you eat it?"

Austin replied, "I dip it and pop it in my mouth, eating it with all in one bite."

"Me too! But it takes my wife at least three to four bites to eat one onion ring! She savors its flavor. Do you see my point, young man?"

"Yes, sir, I do! This kind of wisdom is what my dad and my soon-to-be father-in-law just said they could give me to help me get through times like these. *Tell me more!*"

"Women, too, require a lot of patience as they enjoy getting where they need to be. Austin, do you listen to any country music? Brad Paisley sings a song, 'Waiting on a Woman.' Well, that's what you must look forward to for the next fifty or sixty years, and it's worth it. Also, I've learned that they laugh louder and they hurt longer. I've seen my Sally's tears turn quickly from pain to joy, then right back to pain again before I even have a chance to offer her my hanky. Most of the time she needs me to say nothing, just be there loving her. The best advice that my father-in-law ever gave me, I'm going to give to you free of charge. It's that a marriage has a *no-return policy*. Marriage is *till* death do you part."

"Austin, do you want a few more pickles?"

"That would be nice."

"Carol, more pickles please!"

Their conversation continued with Ben saying, "My Sally makes the best southern pecan pound cake, and you're in luck, Carol serves it here. Thanks, Carol, for the pickles, and when we're done with our burgers, bring two slices of Sally's cake and two cups of coffee *please*. And, Carol, don't give us those thin little slices. We want a couple of thick slices, *ya hear*!"

Austin joined in with a compliment. "Ma'am, that was the *best cheeseburger* that I have ever had. I need one cheeseburger with just ketchup, a small order of fries, and a vanilla shake to go. When it's time, bring me the check. This meal is on me, Ben."

"Well, thank you kindly, young man."

Both ladies were all out of tears.

Sally said to Katie, "My friend Carol owns this place. To most, she's a little tacky and rough around the edges. But she's still a good person and a better business lady. If you don't mind me asking, who or what has broken your tender heart? Surely it's not that good-looking young man you're traveling with?"

Katie showed Sally her emerald engagement ring and let Sally know ... "His name is Austin Tatterson, and he's my fiancé. He's been my friend since childhood. *Oh no*, he's not the problem, he's wonderful!" With that being said…a single tear flowed down Katie's cheek.

Katie walked over and leaned against the pavilion's post. Then she began to read out loud the abortion statistics written on Ben and Sally's sign.

> According to the World Health Organization—every year there are an estimated **40–50 million abortions**. In the United Sates, there are about **1.3 million abortions** each year, which is **3,562 abortions** every day.

"His name was Kurk. He was a better actor than a politician. He fooled me into believing that he was a gentleman. But it was only a part he was playing to get into my panties. Sally, *he raped me!*

"He then married my ex-college roommate, and I just recently found out that they both had drowned on their honeymoon in a boating accident.

"Kurk's craftiness and good looks blocked out all my parents' instructions, as well as my friend Tonie's concerns about him. *I am so ashamed!*"

Sally walked over and hugged Katie, telling her, "You did nothing to deserve what that man did to you!"

"*You don't understand, Sally. He* got me pregnant, and I had an *abortion*. My baby is one of those statistics over there," Katie said, pointing to the sign. "How can Austin marry me if he finds out? And I could never tell my parents. I could never let them down like that! I can't risk them looking at me as their shameful daughter. I can't undo it. I can't even pray it away! God knows I've tried! Sally, do you think this pain in my heart will ever go away?"

"Katie, you may not know it by looking at me, but I too know something about a mother's pain. Ben and I have had three miscarriages. That was years ago, and the pain in my heart has never entirely gone away. But I do believe that the love of our loved ones mixed with *forgiveness* helps us in dulling it some. In my case, *forgiveness* came after I realized that I needed to *forgive God*. I could not go through life being angry at him. *Forgiveness* for me as a Christian was not an option, I just knew better."

"But, Sally, I *forgave* Kurk, releasing him from my heart, to marry Marsha. I too am a Christian, and I too had to *forgive* God as well. But…why then do I still feel so unsettled?"

"Just maybe, Katie, you need to *forgive* yourself too."

Sally walked away, allowing Katie some privacy with God, as Sally quoted Romans 8:1, "There is therefore now no condemnation to them which are in Christ Jesus, who walk not after the flesh, but after the Spirit."

She waited patiently for Katie and God to finish their *quiet time* together.

Katie came over to ask Sally a few more questions that she had hoped she could answer.

"Sally, how can I tell Austin, or should I even tell him? How can I tell my parents, or should I just keep them out of *it*?"

"Child, no one can answer those questions *but you*. What is the *Holy Spirit* impressing upon you to do? Are you really asking me what I'd do if I were you?"

"Yes, ma'am, I am!"

"Well, I believe you need to start out right. You need to tell young Austin the truth. You'll be risking a lot. You may lose him as your fiancé, but you'll probably keep him as your friend. *Isn't your heart telling you that this young man deserves the truth*? All I know is, being man and wife, his heartaches now become yours and yours, his. As well as his victories are yours and yours are his. Anyway, if he's the man you say he is, he'll support you and you both will marry. Then I think it would be wise for the both of you to sit down with your parents and tell them together. Katie, family comes together in times of crises, especially when the family are Christians. Remember that!"

Katie said, "I've heard that a time or two! You're right, Sally, I need to tell him. I've been out here awhile. I wonder how he's doing in there?"

"Well, if he's anything like my Ben, he's been using his fork and spoon skillfully."

"Sally, do you and Ben live around here?"

"Yes, we do, that's our house over there," Sally said, pointing to her farmhouse across the highway. "We live just behind those *3,562 tiny white crosses*."

"So you and Ben must be Christians?"

"Yes, we are! Child, do you believe in divine appointments?"

Katie answered, "I do now!"

"You said you went to Colorado after Austin persuaded you to go. You could have said no, but instead, you decided to take a vacation from what was troubling you, didn't you?"

"That's true," Katie said.

"Well, answer me just a couple more questions, if you don't mind. Do you feel stronger now than you did when you were back in Indiana? Is that hopeless feeling gone?"

Katie answered *yes* to both questions.

"Then you're ready for what's next. Tell Austin about your child. You said you believed it was a girl and not an *it* at all! *Tell him that.* Now, my next statement may or may not surprise you, but here goes. I believe our three babies still *are*—meaning they are alive, alive in heaven, and Ben and I will join them someday. We quit asking why a long time ago, replacing it with, 'Lord, we're just *gonna* trust in you.' To prove to you what I am saying is true, answer me, is your little girl in your heart and on your mind? If so, there is no reason to hide her from anyone. She exists, and that's all there is to it! I believe if you choose to tell that to Austin, he will continue to love her mommy unconditionally."

Just about that time, out walked Austin with Ben.

"Well, well, ladies, is the hen party over, or do we men need to go back inside and eat our supper too? We can do that, you know! Carol chased us out, saying that we already ate her out of house and home. And, Sally, it will be of no surprise to know that Carol gave me a to-do list for this evening. I thought it best to run for it before she put an apron on me too! Isn't that right, Austin?"

"Yes, sir, it is!"

Sally spoke up and said, "She's been known to have us do the dishes a time or two when Joe called off sick, haven't we? She's quite a character, that Carol, isn't she, Austin?"

Austin replied, "Where does she get all of her jokes from? She could really have her own late-night talk show."

"*Shh*! Please, don't let her hear you say that! She'll print up business cards and send a tape to all our local TV stations. And knowing Carol the way we do...*she'll become an overnight sensation*! Then, who would Sally sell her cakes and pies to?"

"Katie, it's been very nice meeting you!"

"Sally...the pleasure has been all mine!"

"Son...do you have just one more minute to spare?"

"Sure, Ben, what can I do for you?"

"Why don't you show me your car. I would really like to see the engine. I hear it's in the rear of the car?"

"It's Katie's car, but I know she won't mind!"

Their men walked over to the bug. Katie took advantage of this last opportunity to talk with Sally in private.

"Do you know, no one ever presented adoption as my possible choice? Okay, I'm no dummy. I know about adoption. But the state I was in, I was not thinking clearly. It was like I was another person! I was beyond stressed, I was conflicted."

"Honey, I see you as a young lady that just fell through the cracks. If the truth was told, you probably weren't ready to go out on your own. You still needed a *watchful eye* and someone to be a *voice of reason* to help you along your way. *Past* is just that, Katie, it's in your *past!* You're now…on the other side of it! We can't undo *most* of our choices, but we can do one thing about them."

"What is that?" Katie inquired.

"Help others in their time of need! That's what! Pray about what I just said. God needs you, and he will help you do just that! And before you know it, *the sting of that memory will be gone.* And as for your relationship with young Austin and your parents, they may not understand at first, but eventually they will come to terms with your choice. Being truthful with Austin is best, *trust me.* This will not be the only hardship you both will come up against. *The best thing* that could happen is that you both know 100 percent about each other, with no walls made up of hidden secrets to hide behind! *The worst thing* that could happen is what? He may choose to leave. If he does, isn't it better that you find out now than later that he's a quitter?

"Just look at those two over there! They look like two teenagers fiddling with your car. By the way, it must run good, making it to Colorado and back!"

"It sure does. It runs like a new one. You want to go look?"

"I sure do!"

Both ladies walked over to join their men.

Ben showed Sally the bug's engine. Austin hugged Katie, looking deep into her lovely green eyes. He sure was glad that the old Katie appeared to be back.

He was questioning within himself, *Where did she go, and what took her there?*

"Well, you two, Sally and I need to get going. We need to feed our dog, our horse, and Sally's chickens before the baseball game's opening pitch is thrown out! Nice meeting you both. If you two should ever find yourselves by this way again, *stop* in for a glass of Sally's sweet tea, and we'll have a good time rocking on the porch."

Austin said, "I'd like that. But I'll have to have another piece of Sally's pound cake." Turning his attention to Katie, he said, "I almost forgot! I need to go back in the diner. Katie, I placed you an order, and it should be ready by now."

Sally hugged Katie and kissed her on the cheek while whispering in her ear, "I'll never forget you and your little girl. Remember, *you're not the worst thing you've ever done!* Get started making those wedding plans, honey."

Ben opened Sally's door for her; she climbed into his truck. They crossed the highway onto Bethesda Acres Farm.

Austin yelled out to Ben, "Don't forget the ladder and Carol's light bulb!"

Katie was in the car.

Austin got in, saying, "No wonder Carol treated Ben like a neighbor, he *is* her neighbor!"

Ben went to over to acknowledge Little Lester and Champ. Then it was on to feeding the chickens, as Sally decided to rock on the porch for a while.

Austin took the keys from Katie and started the car. Then he leaned over and gave her a kiss. She returned it with one of her own.

"Are we ready to go?"

"Yes, I am, but first I need to take you somewhere!"

"Where?"

"It's close by." Katie pointed to Ben and Sally's driveway.

A puzzled Austin pulled in front of the abortion statistics sign, as Katie instructed him to. She pulled a permanent marker out of her travel bag. Then she took her cross necklace from around her rearview mirror. She got out. Walking over to cross number 1, there she placed her necklace around the top of the cross, and with that permanent marker, she wrote "Emmalea" across its top.

Katie dropped to her knees and bows her head in prayer.

Austin felt the need to go over and join her. On his knees, he asked, "Katie, who's Emmalea?"

"Don't you remember? … Emmalea was my childhood baby doll."

"Vaguely I do."

Pointing at the cross before them, Katie explained, "This Emmalea is my daughter, whom I named after her!"

Sally watched them from her front porch. She knew that Katie must be telling Austin all that she had endured. Knowing what was at stake, *Sally prayed*. She watched as Austin and Katie's conversation ended with an embrace. They both got up with joined hands, walking back to the car. They *both* turned one last time to look at Emmalea's cross.

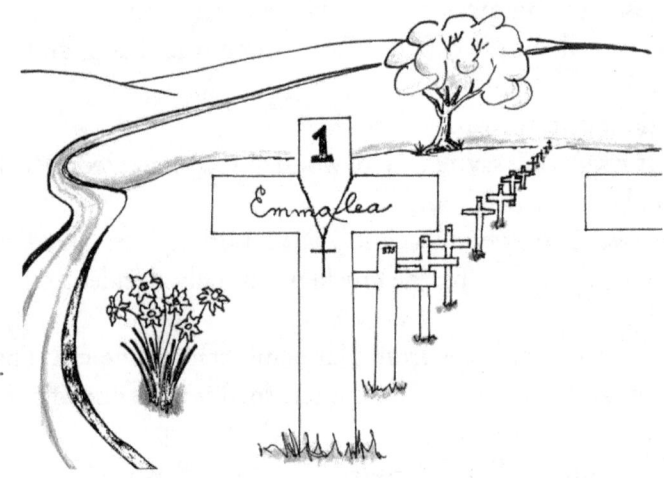

Then they waved goodbye to Sally. She was overjoyed that Emmalea was no longer a secret. Emmalea, too, was no longer Katie's mistake. Most definitely, Emmalea would no longer be called an *it*!

Pulling out of the Bethesda Acres Farm's drive, they were now ready to begin a new life together! Just as their green bug could no longer be seen, Sally's nib-nosy neighbor Carol walked over to see what Katie did to that cross. *As usual*, she was watching from her diner's front window.

What Carol did next puzzled Sally.

Carol walked back to the diner, only to quickly return with something in her hand. Walking over to cross number 2, she wrote "Jennifer" on it, then she hung her favorite silver bracelet around its top. She picked one of Sally's daffodils that were growing along the driveway and laid it at the foot of Jennifer's cross. She quickly wiped away some tears and slowly returned to her diner.

Ben saw Carol crossing the road as he came around the side of the house. He joined Sally on the front porch.

"Honey, walk with me," Sally said.

They both went to see what Katie and Carol had done. They fell to their knees and began to weep after seeing the new additions to *both* crosses. Ben didn't know that Katie had aborted a little girl. They both certainly didn't know about Carol's!

"Jennifer—that's a pretty name, isn't it, Ben?"

Ben said, "Yes, it is. Emmalea is too!"

From that day forward, visitors would come and walk through the Rogers' field of crosses. Most would write their child's name on the cross, leaving a little something on it that would forever connect them to their little one again—*just like the umbilical cord they once had shared.*

That summer, it was on a Friday. When a woman pulled into the entrance of their drive, she got out and placed *two letters* in Ben and Sally's birdhouse mailbox. Then she walked into the field of *3,562 tiny white crosses.* As always, Sally respected the visitor's quiet time. She waited until she left to go and see what the letters had to say.

The first letter was from a lady named Tonie. The second letter was from Katie! Quickly she opened Katie's letter first!

Dear Sally,

God's best for me was right in front of me my entire life. You'll be glad to hear that Austin and I were married on June 4th. He took me to New York for our honeymoon. We saw a Broadway

Musical named *Cats* and we met Donald Trump when we toured Trump Towers.

When we talk about you, I refer to you as my "earth angel." Thanks again for clarity when I desperately needed it the most.

You were right, my parents have worked through their disappointment. You were also right about something else, "**I'm not the worst thing I ever did**!" All distractions from living a good life are now gone. With them went all hopelessness as well.

When Austin and I returned to Alabama, food even tasted better and the sky appeared bluer. Choices got easier to make. Each day was not just a square on my calendar. To the contrary, each new day was full of opportunities to shine! You'll be glad to know that Austin and I are plugged into the young couples group at our church.

We encourage as many as we can by telling them that "God gave us our lives, not just to endure, but to live, really LIVE!" Austin sends his love to you **both**! And as we are busy making memories together, we pray that they'll be sweet ones, like yours and Ben's and our moms and dads' have been.

Love,
Mrs. Katie Tatterson
(555-278-3972)

P.S. Call me to let me know if I can put our story—yours, mine, and Emmalea's on Facebook. As you thoughtfully suggested, I believe it's time to begin reaching out to others—other mothers in need just as I once was. And, Sally, if you ever find yourself needing help with your ministry, *"I'm all in, we're connected!"*

Opening Tonie's letter, Sally read:

Dear Sally,

You don't know me. Let me introduce myself. My name is Tonie Cameron. I'm a close friend of Katie Vincent Tatterson. She told me the story of what you did for her and Emmalea. She encouraged me to come by for myself and my two babies. Cross #18 belongs to my son, "Eric." I named him after Eric Clapton. Cross #19 belongs to my son "Joel." I named him after Billy Joel.

You may be wondering, and asking yourself, how Katie knew her baby was a little girl and how I know my two were boys, the only answer I can give is, WE JUST KNOW!

Thanks for remembering them. I'll forever be grateful!

Tonie tcgbcafe@gmail.com

P.S. If it's OK with you and your husband, Can I come by on their birthdays? It would mean a lot to me!"

Sally went back inside, walking over to her bookshelf, removing her unfinished scrapbook from the shelf. She turned to the page where it looked like her family had stopped. There she placed Katie's and Tonie's letters.

She then sat down at her desk and opened *that* new journal. *Now* she was ready to begin telling the stories of the *3,562*!

Cross no. 1. Her name is *Emmalea*. She would have been Katie's best baking protégé … and an older sister to two brothers.

Cross no. 2. Her name is *Jennifer*. She would have been an honor-roll student, but most importantly, she would have been instrumental in the process of smoothing out *all* her mother Carol's rough edges!

Cross no. 3. His name is *Stanley*. He would have dedicated his life to find a cure for cancer.

Cross no. 4. His name is *Dwight*. His twin sister is cross no. 5. The two would have been inseparable.

Cross no. 5. Her name is *Dolly* (Dwight's twin sister). Both would have been adopted by Doc and Mrs. Coffendatter. They were an answer to both of their prayers.

Cross no. 6. Her name is *Sunshine*. She would have been named that because of her beaming smile and refreshing personality, bringing joy to so many others with Down syndrome. She was not defective after all!

Cross no. 7. His name is *Winston*. He would have been a best friend to many, especially to his grandpa with Dementia.

Cross no. 8. Her name is *Cheryl*. She would have given her mother five grandchildren and came home every holiday and birthday…not missing one!

If you have a little one in heaven or know of someone who has had an abortion, simply write the child's name beside their cross to honor and acknowledge their life. Include a statement about him or her that you believe could have been achieved.

Cross no. 9. _____

Cross no. 10. _____

Cross no. 11. _____

Cross no. 12. _____

EMMALEA

Cross no. 13. _____

Cross no. 14. _____

Cross no. 15. _____

Cross no. 3,562. _____

There's no ending to this book. Because lives don't just end.

Promised Recipes

Sally's Southern Pecan Pound Cake

1 and 1/2 cups softened butter
3 and 1/2 cups powdered sugar
1 tablespoon pure vanilla
6 fresh eggs
2 and 1/4 cups flour
1/2 teaspoon salt
1 cup flaked sweetened coconut
2/3 cups toasted pecan pieces

In a mixing bowl, mix butter and powdered sugar until fluffy. Then add one egg at a time, beating well. Add vanilla. Next add flour and salt. Mix well. Fold in coconut and pecans. My secret ingredient is that I add now 1/4 cup of pure maple syrup. Pour into tube pan. Bake on 325 degrees for 1 hour. Let cool on a rack. Then invert on a pretty plate. Dust top with powdered sugar. It's ready to be enjoyed.

Mrs. Glick's and Sally's Canned Sweet Pickles

(Recipe makes 4 quarts.)
4 sterilized quart jars with lids
4 quarts cucumber slices

(Soaking liquid)	**(Pickle solution)**	**(Brine)**
2 cups pickling salt	1 cup vinegar	2 cups vinegar
18 cups of water	2 cups water	2 cups water
	1 teaspoon alum	1 teaspoon turmeric
		7 cups sugar
		1 tablespoon pickling spices tied in cheesecloth

Place 4 quarts of sliced cucumbers in a large bowl with a lid. Bring soaking liquid to a boil, then pour over cucumbers. Cover and refrigerate for three days. On the third day, drain off liquid. Cover *cukes* with fresh water, cover with a lid on, and refrigerate for two more days. On the second day, drain off liquid. Bring the pickle solution to a boil. Pour over cucumbers, soak in refrigerator overnight with lid on.

The next morning drain off liquid. Place cucumbers in hot jars. Make brine by bringing it to a boil. Then pour it over cucumbers. Seal with jar lids.

Katie and Mrs. Rice's Lemon Brownies

Mix 3/4 cup flour, 3/4 cup of sugar, and 1/2 cup softened, unsalted butter in medium-size mixing bowl. In a separate bowl, mix 3 eggs with 1 tablespoon of lemon zest and 2 tablespoons of lemon juice. Mix the two together, and beat with a mixer on medium speed for three minutes.

Pour into 8" × 8" baking dish sprayed with nonstick spray. Bake 350 degrees for 23 minutes. Let cool then glaze on top.

Glaze 1 cup confectionary sugar, 1/4 teaspoon vanilla, 3 tablespoons lemon juice. Whisk thoroughly. Top your brownies generously!

(These brownies freeze well too! In the summer, we like them cold right out of the freezer.)

KT Cookies

(Cherry Chocolate Chip Cookies)

8 ounce softened unsalted butter
1 cup brown sugar
1/2 cup white sugar
2 eggs
1 and 1/2 teaspoon vanilla
2 cups flour
1 teaspoon baking soda
2 teaspoon salt
1/2 teaspoon baking powder
1 and 1/4 cup oats
10 ounce chocolate chips
1 and 1/2 cup dried cherries

    Mix in order as ingredients are listed. Do not overbeat. Bake at 350 degrees for 13 minutes.

Mrs. Vincent's Patriotic Cake Recipe

(Please do not share with Aunt Eldee!)

CAKE

3 sticks softened unsalted butter
3 cups flour
2 teaspoons baking powder
1 teaspoon salt
2 and 1/4 cup sugar
3/4 teaspoon vanilla
1 cup milk
7 egg whites

Sift flour, baking powder, and salt. Set aside. In a large bowl mix butter, 2 cups sugar until fluffy. Then add flour mixture and milk (a little at a time). In a separate bowl, beat egg whites and 1/4 cup of sugar until fluffy. Next, fold into flour mixture. Bake in a Pam-sprayed sheet pan at 350 degrees for 35 minutes.

WHITE FLUFFY FROSTING

1 cup sugar
1/2 cup water
1/4 teaspoon cream of tartar
2 egg whites
1 teaspoon vanilla

In a saucepan mix sugar, water, and cream of tartar. Cook over medium heat until it bubbles. In a medium bowl, beat eggs and vanilla until soft peaks form. Gradually add warm sugar mix, beating until stiff peaks form. Then it's ready for the cake. (Remember to always frost a cooled cake.)

DECORATION

Top cake with strawberries, indicating the American flag's stripes. Add fresh blueberries, indicating the American flag's stars.

GOD BLESS AMERICA—LAND THAT I LOVE!

About the Author

BORN IN AMERICA, ROSALYN WAS raised in a rural setting in north central West Virginia. Early in life, her interests in reading, music, and caring for the hurting was evident.

She's known for being lighthearted. In fact, her fervent love of laughter, kept her from crumbling under the day to day burden of growing up in a dysfunctional household.

At the age of 12, she was introduced to God. He quickly became her "Heavenly Father". One that kept her in His loving arms.

God directed her education which included, becoming a Nurse, that she practiced for 35 years. Also, she had the privilege of becoming an Assisted Living Administrator, a Certified Dementia Practitioner and a CPR First Aid Instructor with the Red Cross.

She's currently the Vice-President of Catch the Vision Ministries and a Member of Christian Fellowship. She is also a member SKP Photographer group and SOWERS. She's an active member in Escapees RV Club. Partner with Bible Reading Ministry International.

Rosalyn and her husband of 46 years, both hold ministerial credentials with United Christian Fellowship. They have three grown sons. The best daughters-in-laws that they could have asked for and are blessed with 5 grandchildren.

Recently, she retired from the Nursing Profession, as God again trusted her with a new chapter in her life. Thus, *Emmalea* was penned. Yes, I do mean penned! *Emmalea* was hand written with 30 disposable Bic pens, and 16 legal size writing tablets.

After writing *Emmalea's* first chapter, she learned that only 3 percent of those attempting to write a book ever finishes. It was other's encouragements, God's direction, and her sheer determination not to be counted among the 97 percent that quit, that motivated her to persevere to *Emmalea's* completion.

"Life is not a dress rehearsal. This is our one and only opportunity to do something with it!"

With this thought in mind...*go and live*! Really live! Live a blessed life.

"If you'll only live each day with no preconceived idea on what it should be, but rather, live it as it presents itself...you'll be a much happier person!"

Rosalyn hopes you'll enjoy reading *Emmalea*, just as much as she did writing it.

CPSIA information can be obtained
at www.ICGtesting.com
Printed in the USA
FFHW02n0307080918
48144439-51895FF